Amazon FBA E-Commerce Business Model 2019

$10,000/Month Ultimate Guide – Make a Passive Income Fortune Selling Private Label Products on Fulfillment by Amazon with This Proven Step-by-Step Method

By

Ronald Roberts

Please consult a licensed professional before attempting any techniques outlined in this book.

By reading this document, the reader agrees that under no circumstances is the author responsible for any losses, direct or indirect, which are incurred as a result of the use of information contained within this document, including, but not limited to, — errors, omissions, or inaccuracies.

Table of Content

Introduction...11

What Does Amazon FBA Mean? 11

Selling Products on Amazon vs. Your Own E-Commerce Website 13

What Can Amazon Do for New Sellers? 15

Benefits of Using Fulfillment by Amazon 18

Easy Shipping and Logistics Services........................ 19

Lower Shipping Fees... 19

Returns Handling 19

Award-Winning Customer Service............................20

Storage Space Beyond Your Imagination 20

Fast Delivery..20

Fulfillment Process Handling for Other Channels 20

Downsides of Using Fulfillment by Amazon 21

Most Important Costs and Fees When Using FBA 23

Subscription 24

Per-Item Fee..24

Referral Fee 24

Closing Fees...25

Fulfillment Fees 25

Chapter 1: Creating Your Own Amazon Seller Central Account 27

Amazon Seller Central Account Checklist 27

Business Information 27

Email Address.. 27

Credit Card Information 27

Phone Number.. 27

Tax ID.. 28

State Tax ID 28

Most Important Questions to Ask Yourself Before Creating an Amazon Seller Central Account 28

Must-Have Skills for Amazon Sellers 32

Chapter 2: Selecting the Right Product to Sell ... 37

How Can You Find the Right Product to Sell on Amazon? 37

How to Recognize a Good Product? 38

Affordable retail price, usually between $25 and $50 38

Very low seasonality 39

Lesser reviews for the top sellers 39

Room for improvement 39

Easy manufacturing................................. 39

Finding Products Fast and Easy 39

Comprehensive Market Research 41

Proper Sales Distribution..41

Satisfactory Demand..41

Test Your Competition **42**

Best Selling Categories on Amazon **44**

Chapter 3: The Making of the Products for Your Brand **46**

Selecting the Supplier **46**

Samples Ordering...**47**

Always Test the Sample Before Placing the Order **48**

Placing the Order **49**

Chapter 4: Preparing Your Product for Sale...... **51**

Branding on Amazon.......................................**51**

How to protect and control your brand on Amazon? 52

How to have increased control over your online shop? 55

Advertising on Amazon **56**

Campaign Name 70

Target ACoS...70

Automatic Targeting Type 71

Manual Targeting Type...71

Daily Budget 71

Ad Groups...72

Is it recommended to use both the auto and manual target types of campaign? 75

How to set the campaign budget? 76

SEO Strategies to Improve Your Rankings on Amazon **84**

Product Approach... 87

Performance Approach 91

Anecdotal Approach 93

Opportunities and Challenges....................**93**

Cannibalizing Sales.. 94

Right Way of Selling on Amazon **97**

How Amazon's Buy Box Works? **99**

Professional Seller Account 102

New Items.. 102

Availability... 103

Chapter 5: What Are the Best Ways to Launch Your Products? *108*

Reviews Are Extremely Important.................**108**

Find Something to Boost Your Initial Sales ... **110**

Amazon Coupons..**111**

Follow Up to Get a Feedback **112**

Chapter 6: How Can AMS Ads Help You?..........*114*

Chapter 7: Setting Up an AMS Ads UK Account 117

Chapter 8: How to Get the Most Out of Amazon for Your Business?............119

Getting More and More Reviews............ 128

Generating Sales on Amazon 130

Setting the Right Prices 130

Basics of Amazon 131

Chapter 9: Frequently Asked Questions........... 132

What does Fulfillment by Amazon represent?132

What exactly is the Amazon Seller Central?........... 133

How to open an Amazon Seller Central account?.... 133

What are the fees involved when creating the Amazon Seller account?...................... 133

Is it possible to create an Amazon Selling account for free?........................ 134

What do I have to do in order to comply with Amazon's return policy?........................ 134

How do consumers recognize the Fulfillment by Amazon products on the platform?........................ 134

How to label individual products? 135

How to print labels for your own products?............ 135

Is there a possibility for Amazon to add the labels on your products?........................ 136

How to pack products when sending them to Amazon? 136

How to choose a shipping method and carrier to send your inventory to Amazon?.................................. 137

How to create shipping labels? 139

Is it possible to arrange a shipment of inventory directly from an overseas supplier? 140

How to notify Amazon in advance regarding the products that I'm sending to them? 140

How safe are Amazon's fulfillment centers? 141

How are the feedbacks handled for any sold FBA product? 141

Is Amazon taking care of refunds and customer returns for the FBA products?.. 142

What is the procedure in case of returns?............... 142

How to find the products which have been returned to Amazon and refunded to the customer? 143

Can you consider Amazon as a search engine?........ 143

Is Amazon's search algorithm updated regularly? .. 144

What does Amazon SERP stand for? 144

Conclusion **145**

1. Eligibility for free delivery for the Prime members 145

2. Amazon Coupons and Free Shipping 146

3. Better Rankings 146

4. Seriously Increased Chances of Getting Buy Box 147

5. Trusted by Amazon 147

References..*150*

Introduction

What Does Amazon FBA Mean?

Amazon is one of the biggest online retailers worldwide, which is present in 13 different countries like Australia, Brazil, Canada, China, France, Germany, India, Italy, Japan, Mexico, Spain, United Kingdom, and the United States. It is one of the most diversified marketplaces that sells almost everything on its platforms.

Nevertheless, Amazon is not just a vast e-commerce website. While it also has affairs on television, most of its business is concentrated in the online shopping segment. The company even has premium subscribers - the Prime members - who get a few interesting perks, such as free shipping, special offers, and many more. In other words, Amazon has already created its massive database of customers who do not shop on other websites because of the offers that they have on this website.

Furthermore, Amazon provides plenty of products to all of its users, and many of them get sold either directly or through third-party resellers. The platform shares its success and customers to people who are interested in getting sales. Selling on Amazon can be very profitable for these small companies, especially if they know how to use the power of the brand and its customers to their benefit. Although not all products are suitable to be sold on this platform, any exciting merchandise that a merchant may have can sell as fast as hotcakes there.

In plain statistics, approximately 50% of the sales on this the channel are being made by third-party resellers. There are more than 2,000,000 resellers on Amazon worldwide, and more than 66% of them are using a method called Fulfillment by Amazon (FBA).[1] The rest are using the Fulfillment-by-Merchant (FBM) method. There can be significant differences between these two things.

FBM places the whole responsibility on the merchants, considering they are in charge of creating the product listings, handling all customer-related inquiries, as well as packing, picking, labeling, making deliveries, and dealing with returned items. This is an affordable option for the Amazon sellers, but it does not offer many advantages.

FBA stands for Fulfillment by Amazon. It covers various aspects of the sale and after-sale processes. Furthermore, the platform has a lot of huge warehouses around the world, and they can offer logistics space for the merchants' inventory. Hence, there's no reason not to try benefiting

---

[1] Wallace, T., Goldwin, C., et al. (2019). The definitive guide to selling on Amazon. BigCommerce (p. 122).

from the best conditions that Amazon can offer to your growing business. Aside from that, the platform will do the work for you, including picking, packing or shipping goods to the consumers. It also covers your customer service (the tracking and return part, to be specific) and makes your merchandise visible to all of the users, especially the Prime members, who are usually the big spenders on Amazon. Of course, this service doesn't come free of charge because there is a fee involved for storage, as well as the whole fulfillment process. Many resellers present on the marketplace use the FBA method, but it is genuinely not for everyone. Not only are there some requirements to be met, but there are also serious calculations to be made to establish if this is the right option for you.

Selling Products on Amazon vs. Your Own E-Commerce Website

If you are a small merchant without the notoriety of big players, then you need to think of strategies to increase your sales. Having a user-friendly online shop and running all your transactions through that website may not be the best decision to boost your profits, you see. Despite that, running your business through your own e-commerce site entails that you gain full control over the following:

- Listings and promoted products

- Page designs and content

- Sales, packing, picking, delivery, returns, refunds, and customer service

However, all of the above may not be enough to obtain success; that's why you should know the downsides of managing an online store as well.

- It's possible that the website is not optimized correctly, and you can't get enough web traffic.

- You have a minimal client base since many of your potential customers may not be aware of your shop.

- It's tough to get more significant rankings, ratings, and reviews, so it's hard for people to trust your brand or products.

- When you handle delivery and storage costs, your expenses can be very high.

If you are struggling to boost your sales, Amazon can give you a hand. After all, it is already a successful marketplace. Selling on this platform can be profitable to you. Some of the advantages of being an Amazon merchant include:

- Exposure to more than 400 million users

worldwide;[2]

- Easy way of getting sales;

- User-friendly platform;

- Having shipping, picking, packing, and returns taken care of; and

- Associating your shop with probably the biggest name in e-commerce industry.

When it comes to disadvantages, Amazon may have a few that you also need to consider.

- Higher costs for fulfillment and storage services

- Lack of control over and difficulty in tracking inventory

- Possible more returns.

- Tricky taxation

What Can Amazon Do for New Sellers?

It is essential to understand the value of the services offered by the FBA method. In this case, Amazon offers to:

---

[2] Smith, C. (2019). 150 amazing Amazon statistics and facts (2019) | By the numbers. Retrieved from expandedramblings.com/index.php/amazon-statistics/

1. Receive your inventory in its Fulfillment Centers

In the US alone, there are more than 100 huge Amazon warehouses, and some of them cover more than 1,000,000 square feet (Wallace ete al, 2019). There is plenty of space for your merchandise in these locations. You merely have to mention what kind of products you are shipping, and Amazon will notify you where to send them.

2. Sort and store your goods

Upon receiving your products, Amazon organizes and places them in various areas within the fulfillment center. So your merchandise can be safely stored inside an Amazon warehouse. In the unlikely case of products being damaged while being stored, the company will give you a reimbursement.

1. A customer buys your product on the website. Amazon is responsible for processing the payment and updating your inventory.

2. Everything related to product delivery is being conducted by Amazon workers (or its robots), e.g., picking, packing, and delivering goods to the customers.

3. You can outsource the customer support service to Amazon, which can deliver an exceptional job in this

field. They can easily handle queries related to tracking and returns. As for more detailed inquiries about product information or listing, they can inform you about them so that you can reply to the customer directly after some time.

4. You get paid for your sales every two weeks. Amazon processes payments to your account and transfers your profits after deducting fulfillment and storage costs.

Despite the things that this company can do for you as a reseller, what exactly will you have to do if you choose to sell on Amazon?

Well, first of all, you need to find the right products to put on sale. Keep an eye on your inventory and use marketing strategies to advertise your goods. When it comes to selecting the products to be sold, you will have to ask yourself several of the following questions:

- How quickly can your product be sold? There are also storage fees to consider. Thus, if your merchandise is not selling fast enough, you will be charged a higher storage cost.

- Also, you will have to think about profit margin since this will allow you to pay all the fees involved and may help you earn some cash.

- Checking your stock on Amazon is also something that you will need to do on this platform. Its inventory is something that has to be continuously verified.

- A crucial thing that you will need to do is using the right marketing techniques to boost sales for your products and to make them more visible to more customers on this platform. When there are more than 350,000,000 products on Amazon, after all, this job is essential for your products to stand out from the rest (Wallace et al, 2019).

There are a few essential FBA-related tips and tricks included in this book, which will be discussed throughout the book as well as in the last chapter.

Benefits of Using Fulfillment by Amazon

The FBA option is considered by many specialists as one of the best ways for a small merchant to boost sales. It's tough to think of a different retailer that has more loyal customers than Amazon, considering more than 400 million shoppers are mostly buying on Amazon (Smith, 2019). Thus, any seller needs to understand precisely the benefits of signing up to this program.

Easy Shipping and Logistics Services

If you are doing the fulfillment process by yourself, this can turn up to be very time-consuming, especially if you have a lot of orders. Imagine doing the packing and shipping for all the customers and spending hours on these processes when your focus should be on product marketing. By using the Fulfillment-by-Amazon method, you can externalize these processes and take full advantage of the platform in this field.

Lower Shipping Fees

Amazon can negotiate outstanding contracts with couriers all over the world so that you can send products at a discounted rate. The shipping cost is not reflected in the total price of the merchandise in many cases, primarily if your product is bought by a Prime member (who can benefit from free delivery).

Returns Handling

It would be beneficial if you wouldn't have to worry about any administrative procedures, especially when it comes to returns. Amazon can take care of this aspect for you, as well as manage inquiries, reverse logistics, and return shipping labels. They do charge an extra fee for this service, but it's worth it.

Award-Winning Customer Service

If sales are getting new customers, the support service is what keeps them tied to your product or brand. Amazon can handle this job 24/7 easily over the phone, through chat or via email.

Storage Space Beyond Your Imagination

Using FBA takes a load off your shoulders when it comes to storage space. Thanks to it, you will have more than enough room for your inventory. If your products are selling quickly, then you are eligible for unlimited storage.

Fast Delivery

With fulfillment centers all over the globe, it's no surprise that the products get delivered in 48 hours at max. When a customer places the order, the merchandise is usually sent from the closest fulfillment center.

Fulfillment Process Handling for Other Channels

Perhaps you want to make sales on several other platforms, and you are wondering how to send products to customers who use them. Well, Amazon has a Multi-Channel Fulfillment (MCF) service that allows you to use its fulfillment centers even though you are not distributing goods to an Amazon customer. This service can be easily activated; you can also find out information regarding order updates or tracking information through it. Furthermore, you can send the data to the consumers from a different website.

Downsides of Using Fulfillment by Amazon

Nothing is perfect. Even the Fulfillment-by-Amazon service can be very tricky. Here are a few disadvantages that you will need to consider.

1. This method costs money

In this case, you will need to expect both fulfillment and storage fees. If the latter costs are apparent, you have to be aware of how quickly your products can sell, considering you are also paying for storage space for a certain period. If you understand this particular aspect, you can estimate how much your profits will be.

2. Speaking of storage fees, the long terms ones can be quite expensive

If your inventory is sitting for a very long period (six months, for instance), you can end up with paying incredibly high storage fees. So, you will need to make sure that your inventory is being sold as quickly as possible.

3. Watch out for more returns

Amazon is oriented on customer satisfaction; that's why it

facilitates the smooth return of products. When selling on this platform, you will need to comply with these rules. You may be experiencing test or impulsive buying from customers, which may lead to a higher rate of returns.

4. Preparing a product is not easy

When selling on Amazon, every seller has to adhere and subscribe to a strict set of regulations related to packaging and labeling a product. To be specific, they have to be entered into the database, marked correctly, and sent to the right fulfillment center. It may take some time until you get used to all the procedures for this process, though.

5. Checking inventory may not be the easiest thing to do

Keeping an eye on the available stock is a bit difficult because you can't see the remaining list precisely. Hence, you can get a glimpse of the items that are not selling or the ones which have run out of stock. If you trade on multiple channels, this task is even more challenging.

6. Taxation is hard

In the US, where taxes are different from a state to another, it is bothersome to calculate the sales taxes you owe. You can have your business in one country, but the Amazon warehouse can be in a different state, and it may also shuffle the inventory between warehouses. So, you are probably asking yourself if you have to collect the sale tax in the country you have your business in or in every state where Amazon operates. In this case, you will have to get the services of tax advisors, who can quickly help you resolve this dilemma.

7. Your products can be commingled with others

By default, the Amazon Seller Central Account is set to have commingled products. Meaning, your products can be mixed with other ones, which can lead to situations like a customer buys your product but gets something from a different merchant, which may have a lower quality. There were instances in which some merchants sent out counterfeit or even damaged products. For sure, you don't want your goods to get mixed with such products. This may lead to complaints and negative reviews, which will eventually cause Amazon to ban you permanently. The solution, therefore, is to label your products properly.

Most Important Costs and Fees When Using FBA

There are five types of fees related to Fulfillment by Amazon.

Subscription

The subscription is a fee paid monthly depending on the account type. When you plan to sell on Amazon, you can do this by using a professional or individual account. Based on the sales that you expect to get per month, you choose from one of these two types of accounts. It's good to go for the latter if you assume to have less than 40 sales monthly. This way, you will not have to pay anything for the subscription. On the other hand, if you are estimating massive sales, then you should go with the professional account. The subscription will cost you $39.99.

Per-Item Fee

The Per-item fee is only applicable for individual account holders. It represents $0.99 for every item sold. The subscription fee for a professional account exempts this type of account of any per-item charge.

Referral Fee

The Referral fee can be between 6% and 20% (in most of the cases); the only exception is for Amazon devices, which is 45% (Wallace et al, 2019). This type of payment is strongly linked with the product category, and the common percentage is 15%. In dollars, the minimum referral rate would be zero or $1; only watches and jewelry have a minimum referral fee of $2.

Closing Fees

The Closing fees are variable and applicable just for software, video games, consoles, music, videos, DVDs, and books. These stipends usually vary between $0.45 and $1.35, depending on the category, type of shipment used and of course shipping destination.

Fulfillment Fees

The product's dimensions and weight determine fulfillment fees. These costs range between $2.41 and $10, although some prices were going up since last year.

Overall, your costs should be structured into four different groups:

1. **Direct Costs**, which includes product purchasing and shipping it from the manufacturer or supplier.

2. **Indirect Costs** include a wide variety of expenses like accounting, business travel, insurance, tax, samples, website, and so on.

3. **Fees from Amazon**, which provides fulfillment, storage, returns, referrals, closing fees, sales fees.

4. Costs of **dealing with returns**.

Only by considering all these costs that you can estimate your profits correctly; thus, you need to do your math well.

Fulfillment by Amazon is not a cheap service; as you can see above, it comes linked to different other costs. Nevertheless, there are plenty of merchants who are using this service successfully, and they merely have impressive payouts. If you play your cards right, you can be among the successful sellers on Amazon and have your products appreciated by many online shoppers.

Chapter 1: Creating Your Own Amazon Seller Central Account

Amazon Seller Central Account Checklist

There are a few details that you will have to provide when creating an Amazon Seller Central account.

Business Information

This field is related to contact information, business name, and address.

Email Address

You have to provide an email address that is suitable for such account. It should be already set up as well because Amazon will contact you immediately through the email.

Credit Card Information

Providing a valid debit or credit card is very important. If you offer details for an invalid one, Amazon will merely cancel your registration. The debit/credit card has to be linked to a valid billing address, too.

Phone Number

Since Amazon will also contact you back by phone during the registration process, you will have to provide a valid phone number you can be reached on.

Tax ID

This particular number is significant during the registration process since you will have to give details like your company's federal TAX ID number (in the US) or the Social Security Number. During this step, you will be prompted to do the "1099-K Tax Document Interview."

State Tax ID

You will need to mention in which state or states you conduct your business to get the right state tax ID.

For the last two steps of the registration process, it is highly recommendable to consult a tax advisor or different websites like taxjar.com, avalara.com, and taxify.com.

Most Important Questions to Ask Yourself Before Creating an Amazon Seller Central Account

You should not set up the Amazon Seller Account without asking yourself a few questions.

1. Where you will send the Amazon order returns?

As mentioned before, Amazon is a company that's oriented towards customer satisfaction, and they are doing their best to improve the consumer experience on this platform. This also includes handling returns, considering customers can quickly return a product if they don't want it anymore due to different reasons. As a company selling on this platform, you will need to comply with this policy; that's why the return process is something you will need to consider. In other words, you will either need to care of it yourself or outsource it to an agency like tradeport.com or openedboxreturns.com. They specialize in grading and testing returns, as well as in placing the product on sale again.

Also, you have to think of a person from your company who can handle customer inquiries. Know that you not only have to answer everyone but also reply within 24 hours, regardless of the day of the year (according to Amazon's policy). Therefore, all these essential roles have to be figured out already before even creating the Amazon Seller's Account.

2. Is commingling an option if you choose to use Fulfillment by Amazon (FBA)?

The FBA option provides the seller access to a community of customers (Prime members), who spend more money on their Amazon purchases. This group has more than

100,000,000 members worldwide.[3] However, you are not the only merchant who has access to this exclusive buyers club, given the fact that there are other 2,000,000 sellers in total on this platform, and the majority of them have access to the Prime members (Wallace et al, 2019).

Since you have to make sure that your products get to these customers, you can risk to mingle them with other merchants' goods, which may be the counterfeit versions of your items. The inventory is being sent to the fulfillment centers, where they might mix with the inventory of other sellers. A customer might receive a product as well which did not come from you, might be of lower quality, or even counterfeited. Hence, you have to provide serious explanations to the customer. If they file a complaint, you might also be banned from selling on Amazon, all because of a product which wasn't even yours in the first place. It now depends on you to prevent such thing from happening. When creating the Seller Account, it is "stickerless" by default, so you can commingle with other products from different inventories.

Fortunately, Amazon can give you the option of getting a "stickered" account but ensure to change the type of the account before sending the first shipment to the fulfillment

[3] Reisinger, D. (2019). Amazon Prime has 100 million U.S. members. Retrieved from http://fortune.com/2019/01/17/amazon-prime-subscribers/

centers. At least, this is the recommended way. You can also opt for the "stickered" selection later, but you might be exposing yourself to risks if you have already sent unlabeled inventory to Amazon.

3. Do you intend to use a Doing Business As (DBA) name for your Amazon Seller account?

This platform can allow you to hide your merchant identity from the customers by using a different name on Amazon. This is an option to consider if you don't want brands knowing that you are selling their products online, as well as when the reseller is the brand itself, and they don't want their partners to know that they do direct marketing on this platform.

4. Are your products in a category permitted by Amazon?

This is a crucial aspect as the FBA program doesn't allow all resellers to sell through some categories. E.g., alcoholic drinks, vehicle tires, gift cards, gift certificates and a few other products like pamphlets, sky lanterns or price tags. If you don't dabble in these things, then you're in luck because you can sell a wide variety of products without a hassle. Of course, it's highly recommendable for them to have a higher profit margin, but they should also be sold quickly.

Another fact that requires your attention is your seller catalog on Amazon. It's terrific to have all the goods added to your list within the first 30 days since the opening of your account. This way, you can easily find out if you will have problems with some specific stock keeping units (SKUs) and brands. In case they are inevitable, you may need to change your catalog or close the account, primarily if Amazon is imposing restrictions on the products you are planning to sell.

Must-Have Skills for Amazon Sellers

The Amazon marketplace is comparable to a wild jungle where only the strongest can survive. As a new seller, you have to be aware that there are 2 million other merchants like you on this website, so you have a stiff competition regardless of the products you are selling. To rise above everyone, you need to possess some skills and knowledge to boost your sales and always be in front of the game.

1. Outstanding marketing content to build the best product listings

There are high chances that others already sell the product you are selling on this platform. However, to make sure that your items come first, you will need to work on optimizing the details related to them. Focus on product title and description, bullet points, and generic keywords (for SEO purposes). Also, you should add very clear images, including the lifestyle photo of the product on sale. The main image needs to have a white background and a resolution of at least 500 x 500 pixels, but it's not necessary to place your brand on it.

2. Knowing how well your product is selling and how to prevent running out of stock

If you have a favorite product on Amazon, you need to be aware that you will eventually run out of stock. To avoid this scenario, you need to know how to replenish your inventory. Depending on the products that you usually sell, you can fill it again. If you are keen on selling one-time buys or close-outs, then you may have a tough time to replenish the stock since the products can be difficult to find again.

3. Choosing if you want to sell the same product or diversify

If you're going to trade one product on Amazon alone, you can benefit from some exciting tools like the alert and forecasting tools from Amazon. Alternatively, you may try getting help from the likes of www.forecastly.com.

4. Knowing how to find and deal with the old inventory

The truth is that some of the products may not be very

popular and end up being stored for an extended period in the fulfillment centers. Such goods have to be sold on different selling channels to clear up the inventory in the warehouses since you might need to pay extremely high storage fees for them. The good news is that FBA can easily help you identify the old inventory, while the non-FBA programs force the seller to search by SKU to find the stale stock manually.

5. In-depth understanding of every cost

The majority of the sellers on this platform can understand the necessary expenses related to SKU - level profitability, which leads to an overall result - instead of having a clear idea regarding the SKUs that provide the highest profitability and the products that cost to sell on Amazon. Having a detailed cost situation can help the seller comprehend and put together the overhead expenses and acknowledge that those costs have to be integrated into the total amount.

6. Discovering who sells the same SKU on this platform

Without thorough research, you can end up listing your products on Amazon and discovering that there are plenty of other merchants with the same goods later. They will compete against each other to provide the best price for the product, which leads to low profitability or losses. Before creating the account, therefore, it is essential to find out if the products you are planning to sell are already massively sold on this platform, possibly even by Amazon Retail. If so, you will need to list different products on sale. Furthermore, it pays off to study not only your competition thoroughly but also their merchandise. If you are competing against sellers with low prices, you can't expect to have big profits in this niche. Then, you might realize that it may not be the best category to help you make money.

Furthermore, Amazon only charges a fee after the first 30 days of creating the account, so why should you not use that period to set it up properly? You can create the product offers and start selling to activate your sellable inventory, for one. Even if you don't send any listing to Amazon or sell anything, you can still be charged after 30 days because the account is active. In this period, you need to grow your business perspective on this platform. A good method to make it happen is to ask for feedback.

One of the options is to visit websites like feedbackgenius.com, feedbackfive.com, salesbacker.com, et cetera. They are not free of charge, but at least they are not expensive, so they are an investment worth taking. This strategy can show Amazon that the reseller can perform and comply with the platform's performance and customer-oriented policies.

Chapter 2: Selecting the Right Product to Sell

How Can You Find the Right Product to Sell on Amazon?

Finding the right product to sell on Amazon may not be the most straightforward task, considering selling something that you like may already be sold by others. After all, you are in this game for the profit. To achieve your objectives, you may need to go the extra mile to discover the hidden secrets of selling on this global platform.

The ideal product to be sold on Amazon needs to have high demand associated with low competition to ensure that it isn't sold by many merchants. This is common sense since your goal is to find a niche that meets such a requirement. Having your private label can be a considerable advantage in this case, too, because you can mark your place in the market. You can then go after the potential customers without being bothered by competitors.

In this chapter, you can find all the necessary details related to products, which can get jaw-dropping high profits, how to conduct market research, how to test your competition, and which bestseller categories are on Amazon. When hundreds of millions of products are being sold on this platform, choosing the right goods to advertise can prove to be a challenging task. That's why you have to know exactly what you are looking for in the Amazon catalogue. By respecting the general guidelines, you can also find the best products to sell.

How to Recognize a Good Product?

What is the ideal product to sell on Amazon? How does it look like? What are the main characteristics you need to consider when choosing a merchandise? These are only a few questions to ask yourself at the beginning of this process. Regarding the latest question, you can find some key information on how to recognize the best product.

Affordable retail price, usually between $25 and $50

According to recent studies, this price range is big enough to cover fees on Amazon related to storage, fulfillment, and advertising. This is when you have high sales, and the volume of sales can easily cover all these expenses and guarantee a handsome profit. If the price is above $50, then many of the customers will no longer consider its attractiveness, and the rate of the goods is what people see. Hence, the purchases will drop significantly.

Very low seasonality

Meaning, the ideal outcome is not influenced by season fluctuation of sales. You need a product that can generate profits throughout the whole year, not just during a specific season.

Lesser reviews for the top sellers

Usually, 200 is good value in this case. However, less than 100 would be even better.

Room for improvement

You can analyze the feedback received from the customers and improve your product based on them.

Easy manufacturing

Such a product has to be easily manufactured and made of resistant materials; thus, you probably need to avoid glass. You also have to keep it simple. So, electronics and sophisticated goods are some examples of the things you should avoid.

Of course, these are just guidelines since your ideal product may be different from the other merchants. It's all about knowing exactly what to sell in the niche you choose to conduct your business.

Finding Products Fast and Easy

By this moment, you know what to look for in the massive database of the Amazon platform. However, you will need some proper tools to help you in this challenging mission. You need to find measurable information related to products, such as demand, price, seasonality, sales, rating, dimensions, price, and many more.

The Jungle Scout Web App can come in handy to help you scan the products from the platform using the Product Database extension. Another exciting feature is the Product Tracker, which can enable you to track inventory, sales activity, rankings, and prices over some time.

To make up your mind regarding the products to sell on Amazon, you need to track them for a few weeks before deciding after viewing the report provided by the Product Tracker feature. By doing so, you can get a clear idea about how the product performs. If you want to find a suitable niche with a high demand, a handy tool can be the Niche Hunter feature of the Jungle Scout Web App. This extension analyzes the most frequent keywords to discover in-demand goods. It can display a list with plenty of products that buyers search for as well. Furthermore, the feature provides an Opportunity Score, which is based on a search algorithm called Listing Quality Score (LQS). It is responsible for identifying the products with high demand and extremely low listing. The higher the Opportunity Score is, the better.

The Jungle Scout Web App can also be used with the Google Chrome extension to test a multitude of keywords. This process can also display some impressive results from which you can easily find out the competition levels for many products. Using all these tools, you can come up with a list of 20 products which fit all of your requirements, but these products will have to be tested.

Comprehensive Market Research

Once you made up your mind regarding the products you want to sell, the first question you need to ask yourself is: "How many items can I sell during a month?" The goods which have to be filtered by this query have to respect the following requirements.

Proper Sales Distribution

Meaning, one or two merchants do not dominate the niche market. Instead, the sales are distributed amongst a few sellers

Satisfactory Demand

Satisfactory demand is considered when the most active sellers on this market can easily sell at least ten items per day.

If you can generate ten sales per day or 300 per month, that's an outstanding figure to start with on Amazon. Jungle Scout extension can help you with this research since it can easily display a report after typing a few relevant keywords. Aside from the top merchandisers, it will also inform you of their sales volume, product prices, item demand, and many more.

Test Your Competition

After you have shortlisted the products that you want to sell, the second question to ask is: "What is the competition selling this item for?" Again, the Jungle Scout app can come in handy since it can show you some fascinating information like reviews and score ratings. The reviews are the most important aspect think about when analyzing your competitors since the number can give you a distinct idea about the size of the competition. A high number of review indicates a very competitive market - the kind of category you have to stay away from.

Moreover, the tool can also show you a list of products on demand that have a small number of reviews. This information is pure gold because that is what you need to get into. Excellent opportunities are usually referred to highly demanded products with less than 200 reviews; when we're talking about less than 100 studies, these are unique chances. To do your homework properly when assessing competition, you may need to read its reviews to improve your products before selling them as well. Furthermore, you can use the Jungle Scout app to establish which items will be your secondary products. These are the goods that you can still get some profits out of, but you may need to track the results for at least a week or two. By doing so, you are already one step ahead of your competitors.

Also, when studying your competition, it matters to think about a significant feature: Amazon Best Seller Ranking. To explain this term simply, it refers to the order the products that are being listed on a page. The platform sorts and arranges every merchandise that was sold at least once into a hierarchy, which is the Best Seller Ranking (BSR). Using this indicator and the Jungle Scout sales estimator tool you can roughly calculate the product sales volume of your competitors. To be specific, you can choose the category, the marketplace, enter the BSR, and obtain their sales estimation. Such a tool can provide you with the right information to become one step in front of your competition once you apply the proper strategies and get the expected results. If the items that you are selling only have a few reviews, you can seriously play a significant role in this market niche after making some sales.

To be successful on Amazon, you will need to sell the right

products. To make that happen, you have to be extremely practical and sell what is in high demand and has high chances to be sold. It does not necessarily have to be what you like because there may be plenty of other merchants desiring the same product. Furthermore, you might face a steep competition with more established sellers if you insist on doing so. You also have to be incredibly passionate about the products you are selling because you need to know everything about every merchandise to provide the information that the customers need to see, as well as to improve its quality. That is one way for you to create a well-appreciated brand, which the consumers will want to trust and buy from again.

Best Selling Categories on Amazon

One good starting point to select the right products to sell on this platform is to check the statistics of the bestselling categories and sub-categories. The good news is that it's the kind of information that can readily be found on the Amazon website. Therefore, you can browse through the site's categories and wait for each one to display the best sellers. If you limit your search on the specific sections, you will find the best-selling merchants, who may also be extremely competitive; that's why tackling them may not be the wisest thing to do.

However, if you go further and browse through the sub-categories, you may come across best sellers that are worth your efforts. Some products are merely better sold under a private brand, but the areas that may be for everyone are:

- kitchen and dining

- pet supplies

- sports and outdoors

- patio, lawn, and garden

- home and kitchen

Chapter 3: The Making of the Products for Your Brand

Selecting the Supplier

In the era of globalization, trade and manufacturing have no barriers since the marketplace happens to be the whole world. The development of online retail had a positive impact on the production process because they are linked with each other. Increasing sales also means that a lot more products are being made. Competition is growing like never before; to become more competitive, you need to have some aces up your sleeve. Having high-quality products at better prices is what that is all about. Nowadays, everyone turns to China when it comes to manufacturing practically everything, considering most of the products in use have at least a part being created over there. That's why this country is better known as the factory of the world.

If you are merchant who thinks of selling on Amazon, then you probably have a slight idea of what you want to put on sale. In the previous chapter, we already covered key factors, such as how to find your best-selling product, what market niche you need to approach, what information you need to know about the competitors and the product, as well which bestselling categories are on Amazon. It is now time to find your manufacturer or supplier, and the best location to begin your search is China.

The ideal portal for finding suppliers and manufacturers from China is Alibaba.com. This platform connects companies from across the globe with Chinese manufacturers and suppliers of all kind of products. Alibaba does a huge favor to the worldwide trade as it makes the interaction between all these companies, foreign or not, more effortless than ever. You can easily see what the manufacturers specialize in, along with their portfolio, local address, and contact details. The website makes looking for such information extremely easy because they carefully select all the producers and suppliers that are present on the site. Hence, you can guarantee that all of them are legit and capable of communicating in English or other international languages. This further entails that you can contact several suppliers and manufacturers and inquire about every possible detail related to a bulk order (for instance, 500 units). E.g., key features and attributes of the product, shipping cost, price of the items (either for retail or wholesale), delivery terms and period, and payment terms and methods.

Samples Ordering

Once you have received a few offers, you need to create a shortlist of the most interesting and relevant product providers for you. The next step is to order some samples from every candidate to find out which one makes the most suitable goods for your business. At this point, you should not be looking for the cheapest find because, during this process, you should prioritize the delivery period, as well as the communication between you and the manufacturer when it comes to tracking the sample. You do not have to select the highly priced options all the time, but they should not be the most inexpensive ones either because a meager price can mean lack of quality. If you want to sell private-labeled products on Amazon, you need to take care of your image and branding; that's why you have to come up with an original and high-quality product. In this phase, you basically test a potential business relationship between you and the supplier in the future. This way, if you have a sample that can deliver the goods promptly, meets your quality requirements, and has excellent communication with the manufacturer, then this is the partner you need to select from the Chinese market. Again, the price should not be the main factor to influence your decision. Instead, you need to focus on the other aspects mentioned above.

Always Test the Sample Before Placing the Order

When you order the sample, you already set some clear parameters and features, which the manufacturer has to respect to collaborate with you. Since you have just received it, you can possibly contact different manufacturers and compare their goods against each other and check if they meet all your requirements. You will have to conduct some quality checks and, hopefully, they will comply with all them.

Sample testing is a decisive factor when you want to work with a manufacturer. If the sample that you have selected is for a product that is slightly more expensive than the other one that you have compared it with, then you need to contact the manufacturer and negotiate on the price per unit, depending on the order you are thinking to place. In most cases, the Chinese manufacturers are open for negotiations, so this is the right moment to get the best price for the product that you are planning to sell on Amazon. By getting a better deal, it means that you can be more competitive than other merchants who are also selling similar goods on the platform. Not only does it give you an extra advantage against them, but it also promises a higher profit margin, which you can use to your benefit. For instance, you may offer discounts to consumers.

Placing the Order

The final step in this process is placing the order. At this point, you are ideally satisfied with the sample that you have gotten, as well as the communication line with the manufacturer and the negotiation for a better price. It is recommended to start with a lower amount of units in the first order because you have not tested yet how your product will sell on Amazon. Keep in mind that it may take three to four weeks for the manufacturer to deliver your order; on top of that, you need to account for additional one or two weeks for the items to be delivered to a fulfillment center. Once you see your sales kicking in, you can have a better idea of the number of units that you need to order. After all, you already have clear statistics over sales and figure out what the highest and lowest selling products may be. Hopefully, you will have instant success and constant growth of sales so that you can order more products. Most likely, though, a more significant order constitutes a lower price per unit. The more you order, the bigger profits you might get.

Chapter 4: Preparing Your Product for Sale

Branding on Amazon

After you have decided on what products to sell on Amazon, it is imperative to understand what you have to do to prepare them for sale. This is not only related to packing, labeling, and sending goods over to the fulfillment centers. A fundamental issue is branding since you ought to make sure that you have the rights to sell those products on the platform. After, the items there are being sold directly by Amazon or third-party retailers. When it comes to the former, the commodities are owned by the Amazon company; that's why they have full control over pricing decisions and stock. When third-party retailers are selling the products, everything starts to be more complicated.

In the latter case, there are a few different scenarios worth mentioning:

Unauthorized sellers have attracted much attention lately, as many merchants may still find a way to sell on Amazon, despite having no right to do so. If you no longer have authority over your inventory, and other merchants have access to your product, the marketplace can be extremely problematic. In such a scenario, you will have zero control over pricing either since you don't know who the resellers are and you don't have any influence over them to make sure that they comply with Amazon's requirements just like you do.

The worst scenario for a brand is when there is price transparency, but they have no command over it. This situation takes place when some retailers are selling your products with a slight profit margin. The authorized merchants can't stay in the business when the unauthorized ones have these little prices that the brand cannot even regulate. In plenty of cases, the customers will not care who sells the product, as long as they can get the same quality at a significantly lower price. The bottom line is that if the buyers can get the brand cheaper on Amazon, the brand may not be able to promote well on the platform.

How to protect and control your brand on Amazon?

A brand that sells on the Amazon platform needs to have a registered trademark. Sometimes, however, having the latter is not enough to protect the label from the unauthorized resellers. If you own a brand (and also have a registered trademark on it), you may need to get some legal counseling services to defend it from these unlawful merchants who sell your products without your approval. The downside is that this strategy does not always turn up to be very effective due to the gray market (as seen below).

The gray market is an escape path that the unauthorized resellers are using to make a profit out of your brand. Such merchants all have legal advisors, and they are not easy to scare when it comes to label disputes. They always invoke the "first sale doctrine," which is more of a legal concept allowing anyone in the country to buy a product and resell it wherever and to whoever they want.[4] All these unauthorized resellers very successfully implement this escape path under the protection of the "first sale doctrine" and buy and sell your products without having to worry about legal consequences. Nevertheless, there is a solution that a brand may try as well.

To have full control over your distribution and product sales, you will need to get a trademark, which can easily overcome the first trade doctrine. Through this registration, you can specify how your product is handled and how it gets from the retailer to the customer. This is an option that you can enforce better than the standard trademark. There are approximately 75 different ways to implement and define a trademark, and you can use any of them against unauthorized retailers, to ban the first sale doctrine invoked

---

[4] Stim, R. (n.d.). What rights the first sale doctrine gives to a purchaser of a copywrighted work. Retrieved from https://www.nolo.com/legal-encyclopedia/the-first-sale-doctrine.html

by the unlicensed seller.[5]

By tightening your grip over your trademark, you can:

1. Increase your authority over the distribution process and avoid sending cease-and-desist letters to all the unauthorized sellers; and

2. Prove that the continued sale of your products without your consent is, in fact, a legal issue.

By taking this extra step, this kind of merchants can no longer seek protection from

the first sale doctrine. If you stipulate unequivocal terms in the trademark, it means that these merchants will not be able to find a legal loophole to sell your products for their benefit.

The ugly truth is that probably there are not many brands in the world today that have total control over their distribution, and this lack of power can be regarded as a motivation factor for unlawful resellers to continue their dirty deeds. In many cases, the merchandise falls into the wrong hands and ends up being dealt out and sold without the consent of the company it has originally come from. As

---

[5] United States Patent and Trademark Office. (n.d.). Trademark basics. Retrieved from https://www.uspto.gov/trademarks-getting-started/trademark-basics

the label owner, you are undoubtedly keen on having protection on brand equity, but a distributor does not care about this aspect since since their focis is on getting high volumes of sales. Also, they have no regard about the value of the brand on a long-term period or paying the premium price they ask for in exchange for authenticity. Selling on any different channel should represent a motivational factor for the brand to impose selling at a higher price than the generic products.

How to have increased control over your online shop?

The more you control your selling channel and distribution, the higher the chances are to save your business. As mentioned above, it is hard to find a brand anywhere that has 100% control over their products' destination, but you can eliminate any legal loopholes that the unauthorized merchants might use against you. By doing so, these resellers will renounce to sell your products unequivocably, and you will need to worry less about unfair competition. Furthermore, you will have to make sure that the items that you list on Amazon get the Buy Box option; otherwise, the reseller that you authorize may snag it. Once you have done this, you will notice that the pricing control may be in your hands, and it will become more similar with the rates on other selling channels that are not related to Amazon. If you have strict control over pricing, you can also look into marketing your products in physical stores, not just online, by moving merchandise to offline merchants that you authorize. In other words, gaining control of your Amazon channel can save your business since you can get more distributors to sell at a price that you will be able to manage.

Advertising on Amazon

Amazon is a robust marketplace, a real jungle where only the strongest merchants can survive and make significant profits. This platform also acts as a search engine, so it is highly recommended to have all of your content optimized. Nonetheless, is it enough? Will optimization make your products genuinely stand out from the others? Will they be more visible than the rest? The unfortunate truth is that this action does not suffice; that's why you will need to advertise your products on the platform as well.

Since Amazon has an incredibly competitive environment, third-party resellers have to promote their products intensively to boost their sales. The marketplace is the location where the merchandise are being advertised and also indexed by Google. Advertising is a process that can separate the sales part from your branding section. What you need to understand right from the beginning, though, is that the listings on Amazon are indexed extremely high on Google. They usually appear within the first two results for every related search, and you can discover that even if the results are not very relevant with the keywords, you can still have the products visible to plenty of consumers. However, this special feature cannot guarantee phenomenal sales, especially if your content is somewhat weak.

Some of the e-commerce experts consider that the most significant breakthrough on the platform is the development of Amazon Advertising.[6] They back up their answer with the statement that this option is a double sale.

- The PPC element represents the first part of the sale, which involves bidding on keywords by the Amazon merchants to secure the very visible position on the page. Obviously, this whole process is making tons of money for Amazon.

- The sale of the displayed product is the part when the viewing turns into a sale (conversion). Since the latter is made on the same platform, Amazon takes a fee, and so it makes money again.

---

[6] Robischon, N. (2017). Why Amazon Is the world's most innovative company of 2017. Retrieved from https://www.fastcompany.com/3067455/why-amazon-is-the-worlds-most-innovative-company-of-2017

Amazon manages to get a triple win from this process as it:

- Helps the consumer find his or her best match for the product that he or she is seeking;

- Increases the rankings of the seller based on those items; and

- Asks for fees for every sale and ad posting.

Without a doubt, the promoted products have significantly more sales than the standard ones, although Amazon does an outstanding job in displaying the goods using organic optimization while showing the sponsored ones on top. In the past, Amazon Advertising was not an option commonly used by the merchants. Due to increased competitivity, though, plenty of resellers out there are now using this service. Some of them have even become extremely skilled at it. If you ignore this feature, you will be outranked by merchants who are good at:

- finding keyword opportunities;

- bidding smartly;

- having increased budgets (with parts designated for advertising); and

- using experts for this service.

Nowadays, it is not enough to run ads on Amazon alone as you will need to find a way to maximize their performance. Basically, you need to make the advertisements work for you. Since more merchants are naturally using this marketing option already, though, the cost of advertising and competition have also increased. At the moment, the situation is:

- Amazon has gathered all the advertising choices it can provide under one expanded program at https://advertising.amazon.com/, thus increasing the accessibility of their services for first-party vendors and and third-party merchants. The number of sellers who find such features useful are going up significantly each day.[7]

- Sponsored Products ads can be purchased by all the sellers on the Amazon platform, whether they are using Vendor Central or Seller Central accounts. This PPC-based advertising has become the most popular tool on the channel.

- Sponsored Brand ads (Headline Search Ads in the past) are also becoming more popular because they are available to brand-registered merchants that

---

[7] Amazon Advertising. (n.d.). Retrieved from https://advertising.amazon.com/

operate on Amazon. This options features interesting product placement opportunities that are different than the Sponsored Brand ads but also links to the Amazon store brand page.

- Product Display ads are quite interesting since they can show up on your competitor's page along with product details.

- Bids are simply getting more expensive because the product placement positions are limited while the number of merchants using PPC on Amazon are skyrocketing.

However, do not let all the facts mentioned above discourage you. This service has a great potential and investing in it is definitely worth it. You have to capitalize intelligently on the platform's advertising option to make your money work for you. The most important factors that you need to consider to remain competitive when using this feature are:

- Always look for the keyword opportunities which are not marked by the excessive usage of a term or extremely high bids. It is not recommended to bid on the same keyword as all the others, considering this technique will merely increase the bid dramatically, and no merchant can win because of that. Amazon, on the other hand, makes a ton of money by getting paid for advertising. You will have to rule out the ten most expensive keywords and turn your attention to the ones that can also convert views into sales. There are plenty of tools to discover all these keywords, and they can generate reports on the user search terms. You may also try the reverse ASIN search to look for keywords associated with your competitors and how well they perform. You will quickly master this process and be ahead of your competitors.

- Don't hesitate to spend money to make money. When you invest on something financially, you can expect to get a revenue in the near or distant future. This idea is the same with advertising on Amazon. You will need to provide a capital before you can garner sales and profits. If you have found a keyword worth spending money on, you will need to spend extra to get your product placed in a specific spot. Bid+ might be very helpful if you go on a bid war with a competitor. You are probably trying to control the ACoS, but having a very low figure for this indicator is not something that you should wish for. In case you know that spot will bring you better sales and ROI, then you will need to spend the necessary amount to secure that position.

- Don't count on Sponsored Products ads alone. You may

think of the following instead.

- o Try the Sponsored Brand ads if you are a third-party merchant with a Seller or Vendor account. There is definitely less competition with this option, and you can direct buyers to your brand page on the Amazon store, where they can check out all the information about your merchandise. You are making them aware of your brand and products and increasing your sales by doing so.

- o Product Display ads are not available for Seller Central accounts. They are simply meant for the first-party vendors. The good news is that there is even less competition to see when you use this option.

- o You can mix them up or try them all (if you have access to the ads) to find the winning combination to boost your sales.

- Try automatic and manual Sponsored Products ads campaigns. Mix them together sometimes to have more control over negative keywords and Ad Groups. However, you do not have to think about the automatic campaigns as completely useless; that's why you should not rule them out. You can practically run them and let the Amazon algorithm do its job. It can come up with keywords you have never thought of on its own.

- Use extra tools for advertising on Amazon. Go the extra mile; don't just rely on the options presented by this platform.

Amazon Advertising is a highly dynamic domain that is continuously changing every day. You will have to customize your strategy to get the results that you expect to make your products more visible and boost your sales. It is recommendable to always be informed regarding the latest strategies and technologies that appear on the channel. Since your listings will need constant tweaking and adjusting, you will never have to stop optimizing and testing. Find out everything about Amazon PPC, as well as attend related webinars. Remember that what was working yesterday on Amazon Advertising may not be working tomorrow.

Moreover, you can't discuss Amazon Advertising without mentioning Amazon Sponsored ads, which is included in this feature (more exactly, the PPC/CPC division of this service). There are no less than six divisions under Amazon Advertising, and Sponsored ads is just one of them. It is probably the most affordable one, too, and the most commonly used. The platform pages display premium-auction positions which are designated for these ads. This is where you can find specific ads or brands being advertised.

In order to secure such a position, a merchant will need to bid more than the competitors put in; for some keywords, the highest bidder gets the premium-auctioned positioned. Every time a user clicks on the link in the sponsored ads section, the seller has to pay for that click. There are three types of sponsored ads available on Amazon, and all of them are available for first-party vendors since they are the ones who have a tighter link to Amazon and sell a larger volume of products. They include:

- Sponsored Product Ads

- Sponsored Brand Ads

- Product Display Ads

Third-party sellers can only benefit from the first two types. The second type is merely available for those merchants who have registered their brands with Amazon. It also provides brand protection against counterfeiters. Sponsored Product ads, on the other hand, is a popular and powerful advertising tool on this platform that is not only capable of generating traffic and sales but also overtaking other merchants.

In order to use this tool, you will need to understand what exactly it can do for you. These details can be found below.

1. It introduces a new product to the marketplace

Sponsored Product ads are increasing the visibility of your goods, so you can start selling and watch your profits grow. Once your sales begin to flourish, you will also gain reviews, which are extremely important on Amazon.

2. It boosts your sales and improves your rankings

Having sales will automatically increase your rankings and improve your organic search position. Some specialists tend to call this as the "halo effect" since the advertisement and sales generated using Sponsored Products ads can also raise organic sales.

3. It is probably the best tool to attract new customers

You can't hope for a better tool to attract new consumers than Sponsored Products ads. Once they are buying your products, they can remain loyal to your brand. It entails that you already got them hooked.

4. Sponsored ads are helping you to sell more

In the unlikely event when none of the above applies to you, this tool can still generate more sales. Hence, it definitely constitutes to money that's well spent.

When almost anyone else is using this service - well, not quite anyone, but a seriously increasing number of merchants - you will not only have to run Sponsored Product ads. It is essential to do it better than the rest to achieve your objectives. Chris Perry, a famous specialist in this domain, has named the Amazon environment an advertocracy. If democracy means the power of the people, the latter literally means the power of the advertising. A constant growing trend on this platform is the use of Amazon Advertising, causing the organic search to be less important. A simple statistic (Wallace et al., 2019) shows that more than 54% of the buyers start their product search on this platform, and over 65% of all the clicks remain on the first page. The platform quickly evolves and gets more automated; as the Prime community is getting larger, there is a bigger pressure exercised by the national and private label brands that leads into a fierce competition. If the digital shelf was considered a shelf democracy, the Amazon is literally an advertocracy where you can't survive or exist without paying.[8]

The truth is, if you are not using Sponsored Product ads,

---

[8] Waber, A. (2018). 4 ways brands can win the digital shelf in 2018. Retrieved from https://marketingland.com/4-ways-brands-can-win-the-digital-shelf-in-2018-236906

you are:

- Offering a huge advantage to your competitors;

- Intentionally leaving better spots for placement to your competitors; and

- Saving money while the competitors are getting better sales, rankings and reviews.

If you are currently using the service, then you probably experience:

- Having some rewards, despite spending an awful amount of time going through Excel pivot tables and Amazon reports;

- Spending too much money to outbid your competitors;

- A very frustrating dilemma since you ask yourself who has the most to gain if both you and your competition are using the same data provided by Amazon; and

An ugly truth, considering neither you nor your competitors have the clear advantage, and Amazon gets the most out of it because you are bidding to get the premium-auctioned position, which will lead to increased advertising costs and go straight to Amazon.

What you need to know in this case is that the platform secures your spot depending on your bid and the relevance of the search. It does not charge you for impressions, but it collects a fee for every click that the customers do on your links.

The thing is, Amazon considers Sponsored Products Ads as highly important. They can reveal how companies get their share of "real estate" properties on the platform, whether they are using the designated app, the mobile compatible browser or the full-site from any desktop or laptop. The ads can show up in most of the locations they are considered relevant naturally, looking like the search results generated by the organic search, so the placement advertised also appear as some of the best matches for the keyword search.

The algorithm used by Amazon allows the display of related search results, exact match or similar terms. However, it also takes the advertised positions into consideration, as they are shown first (if they are relevant enough). Merchants should know this when they are bidding on keywords.

Some sellers used conducted some unethical campaigns in the past. To be specific, they were paying people to write feedback about products so that they can generate an immense number of reviews.[9] This practice was already banned in October 2016, but it's still being used by some "feedback farms" who find individuals on social media and convince them to write something about a product to creating a false image about it. Most consumers look for feedback from others when buy a merchandise, you see, and they often gravitate towards the ones with plenty of reviews, especially if the majority of these reviews have 5 stars. Just like these incentivized reviews, the Sponsored Product ads have a similar role because it can assure the best placement on the page and appear in the results for organic best matches.

You have to understand that Sponsored Products ads are all about visibility and integration and that you cannot have the best quality in the world if your products are not visible and the shoppers are not aware of them. A possible explanation is that you have poor quality content, not optimized, which drives your products to the bottom results. You may not even see it in the first two pages, and most Amazon users will not browse beyond the second page of results.

To benefit from all the perks offered by this tool, you will

---

[9] Cracked. (2016). I get paid to write fake reviews for Amazon. Retrieved from https://www.cracked.com/personal-experiences-2376-i-get-paid-to-write-fake-reviews-amazon.html

need to realize how to run a Sponsored Products ads campaign first, as well as what its components are and what it does exactly. Just to make it simple, such a campaign is grouping ads to achieve an objective. Picture it as a bowl in which you have all the products necessary to boost sales and become more visible. It's highly recommendable to use one item per campaign so that the consumers can easily associate the product with the advertising campaign.

When running the Sponsored Products ads campaign, you will need to set all of the following:

Campaign Name

In this case, you will need to choose a campaign name that is both descriptive and effortless to remember.

Target ACoS

ACoS stands for Average Cost of Sales. It is an indicator created by Amazon to reveal the cost-effectiveness of your campaign. In other words, it represents the money you spend on advertising, divided by the revenue generated by the advertising campaign. The lower the percentage is, the better. A good percentage for this indicator would be 25%.[10]

---

[10] Wallace, T., Goldwin, C., Thomson, et al. (2019). The definitive guide to selling on Amazon. BigCommerce (p. 179).

Automatic Targeting Type

You will need to leave the algorithm to work its magic and automatically find out the keywords according to your products and competitors product listing. It's not recommendable to invest too much in this targeting type, but instead just use a small portion of your money to spend on the auto-target campaign, as it can come up with new keyword opportunities (you probably never thought of these keywords).

Manual Targeting Type

Manual targeting is a type that offers increased control over the keywords that you search for. Some tools can suggest you millions of different keywords so that you will only need to set the match type - whether it's broad, phrase or exact match - to maximize your views and eventually your sales.

Daily Budget

Daily budget is the amount of money that you are willing to spend on a daily basis to advertise your products. The recommended monetary allowance for auto-target campaigns every day is $5 to $10. For manual-target ones, you will need to increase your spending and raise the amount at $20 per day in the beginning.

Ad Groups

In this phase, you will need to set important facts like default bids, match types and keywords, and the keywords you want to avoid.

During this campaign, you will need to get familiar with the terminology. Therefore, you should know what the ad keywords or user search terms may be. When you start your campaign, you will have to inform Amazon about the keywords relevant to your product. At this point, you need to phrase them how you consider the consumer will type to find what he or she is looking for.

When you pay for these ads, you will have to be careful with the keywords. If you phrase them properly, your product will show on many searches.

The Amazon terms refer to the words and phrases the consumer use when looking for a merchandise on this platform. The marketplace matches the terms with the keywords that you set and then displays the most relevant products. If you do your job right and formulate them correctly to match as many words as possible then your items will be displayed when the customer is looking for something to buy. There are two ways keywords pair with search terms: auto-target and manual-target match.

The main advantages of the auto-target match are:

- It's fast and easy.

- Amazon comes up with a list of keywords, which are obtained from an extremely vast data collection process.

- It's highly likely to get keywords that you thought of.

Also, you can find the disadvantages below.

- You have a lot less control, but at least the process is easy.

- The process will also generate fewer relevant keywords, and this can affect you.

- Amazon wants to keep this type of match because it generates an immense number of possible keywords, and every word will lead to a click (Amazon is winning money in this case).

A term that you have to get familiar with is conversion (which is the order itself), representing the sale that resulted after clicking on the Sponsored Product ad. The conversion does not mean each sale, as a customer can buy 15 items of the same products, but it still counts as one conversion. In other words, the conversion is the view of a product converted into a sale.

Manual-target search is pretty self-explanatory, and it has

to be regarded as the bull's eye for darts. It has a few distinct characteristics like:

- **Broad match**, which includes the specified keywords regardless of their order, permitting to show other words in between or before and after. This type of match is the widest, but it does not provide the best result. The keywords paired this way may convince shoppers to buy your product or drive them away as the result is not too relevant to their search.

- **Phrase match** represents a sequence of words pairing with the user search terms. It is also the middle ring of the dart's bull's eye since the match may allow some misspellings. Obviously, it delivers better results than the previous one, thus increasing your conversions rate. In other words, this type of match will significantly raise your chances of getting a sale since the product displayed after typing the search terms is more likely to be more relevant to the search.

- **Exact match** is self-explanatory, considering the keyword matches exactly with the search term entered by the customer. This type provides the greatest results because the product displayed is the one searched by the shopper. The conversion rate is extremely high in this case.

- **Negative keywords** are those types of keywords that you don't want to place a bid on. These words should be discovered during this Sponsored ad campaign, more precisely at the ad-group phase.

Is it recommended to use both the auto and manual target types of campaign?

The most effective way of using Sponsored Products ads is the manual-target campaign. This process will result in more relevant data since you have increased control over such data, which will allow you to adjust your campaign easily and optimize it to get the objectives that you are looking for: a higher conversion rate correlated with a lower ACoS. The auto-target campaigns are still useful, especially if you use them additionally to the manual-target ones. If you want to collect a huge amount of data cheaply and without being involved, then the auto-target campaigns are for you. However, the higher the percentage is for manual-target campaign use(in the situation you are mixing both methods), the higher the chances are that you have to obtain the most relevant keywords and user term search, and they can be very helpful for you.

How to set the campaign budget?

As seen above, the manual-target campaigns are the ones with better results, so you should focus your financial resources on it. The manual-target campaign can be compared to a vacuum, while the auto-targeted one is comparable to a broom. The reason is that the former can get you the most number of keywords as it absorbs every important part. Therefore, it sucks in even the "crumbles" of the keywords, not leaving too much behind.

Whatever is left behind (if there is anything) is picked up by the auto-targeted campaign, on the other hand, so it sweeps the remaining bits left from the keywords; thus, it's compared to a broom. Without any doubt, the vacuum collects the most important results for you - not the broom - and so you need to focus your budget on a manual-target campaign. You also have to set a daily cap when it comes to spending on campaign and configure your default bids for keywords levels and more specific ad group.

To recap, you can find the key aspects of the Sponsored Products ads campaign on Amazon below, along with their definition or explanation.

- You will need to know that the campaign represents the highest level of grouping within your Sponsored Product ads process. Picture it like a container or a ship containing one or even more ad groups. At this point, you will need to set the daily spending limit, auto or manual-target type, and keywords that you want to avoid.

- Ad groups are part of the advertising campaign. They are considered a smaller container within the larger one. Hence, you can set default bids, match type and keywords, negative keywords, and product ad links.

- Keywords are the bits of information you expect the customers to search on this platform. Such keywords should be based on terms and phrases that the consumers type on Amazon. You can bid on keywords - the ones which you consider that are most likely to be typed in - as well as use the default bid at the ad group level or select a bigger amount to spend on a specific keyword. There are a few types of when it comes to keyword matching, such as:

  o Negative keywords - the keywords that you need to avoid;

  o Auto campaign - a distinct process in which the algorithm automatically provides a list of keywords according to the competitors' products, image recognition, and your own content.

o Manual campaign includes three different types of matches:

   ▪ Broad match is a wide match, not recommendable or usable;

   ▪ Phrase match can be about any matches found by the algorithm with your content, competitors' products, and possibly even image recognition; and

   ▪ Exact match is self-explanatory because the keyword matches the search term typed in by the customer.

• Related Product Ads are some of your products, which can be complementary with the goods that the customer is currently searching. This type of campaign can prove to be helpful for the merchant.

One of the most important features of the Sponsored Products ads campaign is the bid itself since this feature is a form of pay-per-click (PPC) advertising. It means that you are charged for every click made on your sponsored products, regardless if the customer makes a purchase or not. On Amazon, you - as a reseller - are not acquiring clicks; instead, you are trying to outbid your competition when it comes to placing ads and becoming a lot more visible. The boosted visibility can convert a click into a sale. In this case, the bid is the amount of money you are willing to pay for every click made on your sponsored products. When launching the campaign, you will need to establish the bid amounts (financial limit) first on each keyword set at the ad group level.

The starting point in this case will be a suggested bid (also known as the recommended value of the bid), taking into consideration how many competitors there are for the same product and how much they spend for the keyword to win the ad placement. This option can prove to be helpful since it can give you a glimpse about placing ads and the best rates. Ads placement in most cases will not be enough because Amazon is a competitive marketplace in which you will need to always be two steps ahead of your competition. You have to acknowledge that your competitors are getting the same suggested bids, so it's up to you to find the best solutions to stand out from the rest. Using Ignite at this point can help you in your competition, considering the suggested bids have resulted after in-depth analysis and collection of historical and real-time user term search. It can be the ideal tool to place smarter bids and get more ads.

Under normal circumstances, if you bid higher than your competitors, your product will be shown instead of theirs.

However, this is not necessarily a rule of thumb since there are a few situations when the highest bid will not make it to the auctioned position. Amazon already has statistics on any of the products sold through its platform and, in some cases, the highest bidding product will not make it on the sponsored position. How is this possible?

Well, if Amazon is trying to sell a product as fast as possible to generate a higher customer satisfaction level and fewer returns, then that product will become prioritized over yours even if you have the highest bid on the premium-auctioned position. You simply can't beat Amazon when it comes to keywords since it will always have better keywords than yours and will place its product in front of yours. When displaying the sponsored ads or any other products, the platform establishes the relevance and quality of an ad, and you can see how they are doing this below:

- It removes an ad, which is not eligible for Buy Box.

- The remaining ads are simply analyzed using the relevance criteria. (Category plays a major role in these criteria since a product which is not listed correctly will be considered irrelevant). Then, the ads are ranked according to bid value, as well as the probability of the ad being clicked. (Click-through rate is an extremely useful indicator.) There is a mathematical formula for the position of the product Bid Value x CTR. The higher the result, the better the ranking is.

The classic bid has become a popularly used feature during the PPC campaign. Thus, in some cases, it can prove to be not enough. Amazon already has the solution for this scenario in the Bid+ feature. Using this feature sends a very clear message to the platform that you want the top spot; you don't want to settle for less, and you are willing to pay for it. Bid+ allows you to increase your bid value by up to 50% on a specific keyword or ad group. The clicks will be more expensive; hence, it will consume your daily budget faster than the standard bid. At this point, you can adjust your monetary allowance, so you can benefit more from this feature.

During the manual-target campaigns, you will need to understand terms like cost per click (CPC) and click-through rate (CTR). The former represents the amount of money spent divided by the number of clicks covered by it. This indicator shows the amount of money that you need to spend on a click. This value is always below the bid, considering the bid is the maximum amount of money that you can afford to spend per click. Cost per click is a crucial thing to help you discover how much you need to pay for clicks, as well as return on investment (ROI). If the CPC level is higher, it can only mean that the keyword is popular and that your competitors are also bidding.

On the other hand, click-through rate (CTR) is all about clicks and impressions. While the click is self-explanatory, the impressions refer to the number of times that the ad is shown to the shoppers. CTR is an indicator expressed in percentage, which divides the number of clicks by the number of impressions. Its value is different from a category to another, but a normal value will be 0.5% in most cases. When you have terms, which are extremely the value of this indicator is around 5%. Broad-match terms have the CTR value up to 1% (the majority of them), whereas in most CTR cases, the value is below 3%.[11]

However, there are still some other things to consider in the Sponsored Product ads Campaigns, such as reviews and product price. When analyzing what items to display on the sponsored spots, Amazon has to decide which goods are more desirable because they are mostly oriented on achieving customer satisfaction. A product with a lower price and five-star reviews can beat a merchandise that is more expensive and less reviewed, although the second product may have a higher bid placed for the auctioned

[11] Wallace, T., Goldwin, C., Thomson, J., et al. (2019). The definitive guide to selling on Amazon. BigCommerce (p. 187)

position.

When doing a Sponsored Products ads campaign, you need to set up your objectives right from the start. Below you can find some questions, which might help you set your objectives:

1. Are you a newbie when it comes to Sponsored Products ads campaign? Are you trying it for the first time because you are suspecting that your competition is using it?

2. Are you about to launch a new product?

3. Are you trying to get a higher conversion rate on a product which doesn't deliver the expected results?

4. Are you trying to decrease ACoS below a specific level?

5. Do you want to spend less time and be less frustrated on Sponsored Products ads?

6. Do you want move up your rankings by 50 positions?

The answers to the questions above can be sufficient reasons to approach the Amazon Advertising program, but you have to set some goals first, as well as a period of time during which you plan to achieve those goals.

SEO Strategies to Improve Your Rankings on Amazon

Amazon takes special care of the companies with trademarks, providing them with a special place on the platform. Using a program called Brand Registry, which shows on the Amazon, any brand with a trademark can submit items to the channel and lock it down (to protect it). By doing so, you are significantly decreasing the chances of having your products being sold by an unauthorized reseller, who might sell counterfeit or a completely different product and show up as yours - a situation which can cause serious problems to you. This scenario might happen at some point, but you need to make sure that your content is of high quality and fully optimized.

The most important thing that you need to know about Amazon is that this company is customer-oriented and is keen on selling products to these consumers achieve satisfaction and loyalty. When it comes to this platform, another important factor to understand is that it plays the role of a search engine, so you can compare it to Google. The major difference between Amazon and Google is represented by the custom search algorithm. Amazon's search algorithm is named A9, which is designated for this selling platform. People don't pop in on this platform for product research just to find products and read reviews about them, and this is something that Amazon is very much aware of. The platform is constantly adjusting and tries to come up with more desirable products, considering one of its main goals is to boost the conversion rate. The whole process of making the merchandise more visible on Amazon is called SEO, which consists of a large number of techniques and strategies to tweak and optimize your content. The main purpose is to achieve better rankings through organic search and, of course, to get more and more sales.

When optimizing your content for Amazon listing, you will need to consider:

- the quality and quantity of product images;

- the title that it should contain; and

- the price of the product.

Bearing Amazon's philosophy in mind when it comes to caring about customers and selling products to them, you can have great success on this platform. The A9 algorithm is a powerful tool for displaying results according to the words or phrases entered by the potential buyer (search terms). As already mentioned in this book, the match between search terms and keywords set can be broad, phrase or exact. The algorithm really displays results which are relevant enough to the search term. Lately, it was tweaked to display results even though it has misspellings. Also, the search algorithm is developed to show variations as well, which can prove to be helpful since it displays relevant and similar results for a simple variation.

The most important aspects that you need to consider when optimizing your products on Amazon are:

- Visibility

- Relevance

- Conversions

Amazon gathers a huge community of buyers, and it offers you an opportunity (as a merchant) to expose your products to this community. These people may as well be your potential customers, but they will need to find the products you are selling before buying any of them first. To look for a merchandise, they will need a conduct search, which is the most important and frequently used method to find products on Amazon. Interested shoppers will type in keywords which can match your title, description or any information related to your product. At this point, the order of the goods displayed is influenced by factors, such as price, text match, availability, sales history, and selection. In order to rank higher in the list of results, you will need to provide complete and relevant information about the product. This will naturally lead to the merchandise having boosted visibility and seriously increased sales.

There are three different approaches when it comes to optimizing:

- product approach

- performance approach

- anecdotal approach

Product Approach

The product approach is simply about the optimization of your product listing. First things first, you will need to optimize your listing title. The latter should contain all of the following elements: type, line, brand, color, size, material/key feature, quantity, and packaging. The trick is how you choose the order of these elements by considering the additional keywords. Nobody can deny that keywords choice and order can seriously affect the product listing rank. The title of a product displayed on Amazon may have a different number of characters, depending on where it's displayed. On the organic search section, it has between 115 and 144 characters; in the sponsored ads section, it has around 30-33 characters; and on the mobile versions, it comes up with 55-63 characters.[12] From this, you can learn a very important lesson since all these results tell you to put the relevant keywords first in the title. By doing so, your title will be more practical and relevant. It's highly recommendable to have a list of keywords and place them in the title before each character breakpoint. Amazon emphasizes the importance of brands a lot, so it's indicated to start with the brand name in the title.

There are some tools you can use for the keywords, but the main steps that you have to take when optimizing your title can be found below.

1. Make sure you use Magnet to conduct research on two or three of the most popular keywords applicable to your product.

2. Try to find the keywords that your competitors are using. In order to discover them, you can run an "Extensive Reverse ASIN" using Keyword Inspector or ASIN Lookup Tool.

3. Target your competitors with the most reviews. They are obviously in this business of selling on Amazon a lot longer than you are, and it's helpful to find out what their customers are thinking about the

[12] Wallace, T., Goldwin, C., Thomson, J., et al. (2019). The definitive guide to selling on Amazon. BigCommerce (p. 92).

products purchased from your competitors.

4. Gather three to four sets of data, mix them, and eliminate the search terms, which are not relevant to your product. Then, you will need to write your title based on a word or two-word phrase frequency.

When putting keywords in the title, you need to make sure that the title is readable and that it's not a meaningless compilation of keywords. No buyer is attracted to such a title. To make sure you integrate very relevant keywords in your title in a natural way, you can use tools like Helium 10 Scribble Tool. The use of special characters may help you add some style to the title and break up the phrases naturally.

The use of bullets in your title will help you not only with the conversion rate or the relevance but also the ranking of the product. Amazon values a well-structured product content, and the buyers much appreciate such aspect. The most common use for bullets is to present product features or benefits. The words displayed after them are easily indexed by the A9 algorithm, so this is definitely something you need to consider. Keywords which were not used in the title should appear in the bullet section. You can use the Helium 10 Scribbles tool to improve the content of the bullets section. A good use of this section involves compatible products; in this case, you can hit the jackpot as your merchandise can be displayed when a buyer is searching for the compatible product shown in your bullets section, and the chances of sales may seriously increase. Although the former does not influence your rank directly, everything mentioned above just proves its importance.

Nobody can ignore a great story. If your product description is written as a story, it will become more attractive to buyers. Use some keywords in the text (naturally, not forced) and end up your product description with a call to action. Expressions like "Buy Now" or "Order Today" are catchy enough to add. When creating your item listing, you do want to keep it simple, so it is highly recommendable to use simple HTML. However, you have compiled a massive list of keywords because you don't want to miss anything from the search terms that are typed in by the shoppers. You may use the most relevant ones in the title, bullets section, and product description, but you simply can't squeeze them all in there because it will merely be ugly and the text will have no meaning. In this scenario, you will have to put the remaining keywords in the backend, out of sight from the buyers. The keywords shown in this section don't require to be separated by any comma (just use space), and they don't have to be duplicated (because they should not show up in any other section of the text).

Performance Approach

The performance approach is about the strategies used to get better rankings. The most important ones are sales and reviews. Nothing increases your rank like the sell - this is the most powerful way to get a better position in the Amazon results listings. Right from the beginning, you need to acknowledge your place on the marketplace because your merchandise may be displayed on page 18, and most of the customers are not interested to browse the first page of results further. The question that you need to ask yourself is: how to generate sales in this case?

You will have to steer internal and external traffic to your listings. Internal traffic can be achieved by Sponsored Products ads, while the external options refer to the ads on Facebook (or other social media websites), Google AdWords, and so on. Some strategies in this case (external traffic) may involve advertising on Amazon listings, as well as on the pre-sale pages. Other methods deal with ads to use a discount code delivered by email in the squeeze-page for opt-in single use discount code or advertising on the product sales funnel.

Using a launch service is also something you can try as long as they don't violate any terms and conditions on this platform. Viral Launch can be the right tool to use because they can help you move the product up in the rankings and have a great customer support service.

It always helps to remember that Amazon is a platform which values customer satisfaction; that's why the reviews here are highly regarded by them. Getting a large number of reviews is probably the second most powerful tool to boost your rankings in the Amazon listings. Any buyer likes to be fully informed when making the purchase; thus, finding out the opinion of other consumers related to the merchandise can influence their decision of buying the product. In the past, some merchants were using unethical methods to get more reviews. They were merely paying people to write plenty of positive reviews for their products, to be specific. Amazon tried its best to eliminate the fake reviews because they want to avoid any false statement related to products. (This is how much they care about their shoppers.) First of all, reviews are social statements related to products, and they can provide valuable information to the potential buyer, hence influencing them to purchase or not purchase the merchandise. Secondly, reviews are boosting rankings. Everyone wants to have their product on the first page, but you can achieve that by getting reviews (real ones). Developing a close relationship with your customers can help you get more of that. You can use tools like Sales Backer and Feedback Genius as well to compose custom emails for your clients to receive their honest feedback after buying your product.

Anecdotal Approach

The anecdotal approach includes tips and trick on how to optimize your content on this platform. These are advices that are not documented by Amazon. You can find them below:

1. Try using FBA.

2. Don't hesitate to use brand names in your product listings.

3. Don't forget to include the seller name.

4. Complete other fields in the edit product page.

5. Use quality photos in order to improve your rankings and conversion rate.

Opportunities and Challenges

Right from the beginning, you have to set the right expectations because, realistically speaking, your product will most likely not sell like "hotcakes." There are more than 400,000,000 products on Amazon, so to stand out from all these products is not an easy task.[13] You will need to customize strategies in order for your products to be noticed by a larger number of consumers. You have to think about solutions to generate traffic to your listings. You can use Facebook, pay for advertising on Amazon, or send emails to your customers, informing them of your presence on the marketplace. You can find some myths or strategies of selling on this platform below.

Cannibalizing Sales

This is a myth which, in most cases, does not have any real support. Plenty of brands are worried that they might be cannibalizing the sales from their own websites if they are selling on Amazon. This concern is merely false because it is hard to think of any brand, which has a wider customer base than Amazon. When you have access to hundreds of millions of consumers, there is no other place to be than this platform. The sales made through this platform will most likely be higher than the ones made through your own website. If you spent plenty of money on advertising via Amazon, this is most likely money well spent because you will be facing sales unlike any other platforms. The traffic generated on Amazon is merely beyond imagination, and you have the chance of getting a portion of this huge traffic

---

[13] Wallace, T., Goldwin, C., Thomson, J., et al. (2019). The definitive guide to selling on Amazon. BigCommerce (p. 68).

to your listing. It's no better way to make your product more visible and boost your sales. No matter what product the consumers is choosing, Amazon wins anyway because it doesn't care about your merchandise in particular when there are probably ten similar products, and one of them is going to be sold. You can choose if you want to get a small piece of a huge or whole pie from your own site. There are many brands that choose both because they are aware of Amazon's value. They can set this platform as the main selling channel and then the official website as the secondary marketplace. Also, some of them have realized that the latter is more for presentation than selling, and Amazon is the place to be if they want to have sales through the roof. If the competitors are already doing sales on Amazon, then they probably shouldn't hesitate to go on the platform.

However, you as a merchant will not have to rush and jump in to make sales on Amazon. You need to test the platform first to find out if it works for you or not. You can use a few products in the beginning to track their progress and closely follow up their performance. This strategy is called by some specialists as the dip-the-toe-in method. When you conduct most of your businesses through your own website, and you are curious about how Amazon can work for you, it is highly recommended to try a few products first on this platform to check how they are performing. Choosing the right merchandise to be sold was already discussed in a previous chapter of this book; after considering all the advice from that chapter, you can try a few products on Amazon. Preparing them before selling also involves optimizing the content because having high-quality content is only a step to help boost sales and generate traffic to your listings. That's right! In order to have results, you have to do this process correctly! Although it's a good idea to start with one or two products, having a wide variety of products on Amazon is not a bad idea since you will definitely have more customers on this platform than on your website. Since you are adding your merchandise to a database where there are already 400,000,000 products (Wallace et al., 2019), you have to make an extra effort to generate traffic and make your products visible to customers on Amazon and get sales. You always have to keep in mind that there are more than 2,000,000 third-party resellers already on this platform. If you consider the top 1%, they all know how to play this game very well, and they have been tweaking their content and updating their strategies to boost sales. Such merchants understand how to source products in Asia, recreate a product, bypass trademarks and patterns, and develop a product that is similar to yours, but the consumers can see their merchandise because they have excellent rankings. In the meantime, you are probably spending around $100 per month to lure 20 people to your listings.

The problem of unauthorized merchants will not disappear by itself, so you will have to protect your brand from these unfair practices. Ignoring the problem is exactly what it's not recommended in this case. If you don't take measures against this issue, it will affect all your selling channels and eventually lead to destroying your business. However, although you are facing this problem, it does not mean that you need to exclude Amazon as an online marketplace, especially when your competition is already present on this website. You probably conduct your business through your channel and have a few distributors that generate a few sales. If you are satisfied with this situation, then you are losing the big picture. Amazon will be present for many years to come, and you need to embrace the idea that some merchants may be looking to counterfeit your products, but this is a risk that you will need to take to get benefits at full scale on this platform. If you are selling outside Amazon, then probably some merchants on this platform is already making more money than you while selling a counterfeit version of your product. In this case, you need to get on this platform as soon as possible and make your product available for all the Amazon's consumers.

Right Way of Selling on Amazon

The ideal situation for a brand is to have full control over the pricing. In order to achieve that, it needs to have total authority over distribution as well. To be able to do that, such companies have an ace up their sleeves, a proper trademark which will prevent any unauthorized reselling (at least legally). However, if your product is successful enough, visible, and generates many sales, then Amazon Retail might already be considering to buy your product. In that sense, they approach the brand directly and negotiate a massive sale of this merchandise. Such items are happy to sell a large volume of products, although the goods are sold at a discounted price. Amazon Retail may not be interested to get profits from selling the product; they are most keen on satisfying customers.

If you are already marketing items through Amazon directly, you might also consider selling products on the platform. This business model is also known as the hybrid model when some of them are part of the Amazon catalogue and you also sell products independently on this platform. For your best-selling items, there are high chances that Amazon will find a way to source your merchandise whether you go straight to your distribuitor or search for a distributor overseas (most likely from China). You don't have control over the distributors, so you are being left out of the discussion, and you can't prevent this from happening. A successful model is to sell to Amazon directly, as well as on your own on the platform, because you will have access to different marketing strategies, and you are likely to get impressive sales.

The advertising tools designated for first- and third-party sellers have the purpose of generating traffic to your listings, which can lead to significant revenues. The only information that you get from being a first-party reseller is the number of units sold. For third-party resellers, these tools can offer more details regarding the units sold for each product, along with other precious information, which can help you collect more data regarding consumers. As a third-party reseller, you can enjoy more flexibility and decide to play a bit with the products you sell. You can create bundles and make the products more attractive to customers. The hybrid model is probably the best way to conduct business on Amazon.

How Amazon's Buy Box Works?

Buy Box is the tool that you can use on Amazon to get your products purchased. More than 82% of the total sales on this platform are done using this button, and the percentage is even higher for purchases made using mobile devices.[14]

---

[14] Wallace, T., Goldwin, C., Thomson, J., et al. (2019). The definitive guide to selling on Amazon. BigCommerce (p. 74).

This platform has more than 2,000,000 resellers who are competing against each other and Amazon itself. Not all the resellers have the option to use Buy Box because the competition is fierce, and so they have to be differentiated somehow. Buy Box is located conveniently on the right side of the product detail page where the shoppers can merely add to cart the products that they want to purchase. Getting the Buy Box is a privilege since only the resellers with outstanding metrics have the chance to get this coveted prize. You will have better chances of winning this feature if you can understand better than the rest of the competitors how the A9 algorithm works so that you can focus on improving your content. Over the years, the rules have changed, and the Buy Box has become more exclusive; that's why not many resellers can benefit from it.

As the competition is getting tighter, Amazon has removed the one-click buy button from the listings as well where the product is displayed at a lower price than its platform. Instead, such listings will display as "See all buying options."

Merchants have the option to put a price for their products on this platform, but Amazon also has the right to exclude that offer if one item doesn't have a competitive price. Customers can get different product listings on a specific search, but the merchandise with a non-competitive price may not be shown. A metric indicator which was used to offer the Buy Box was removed from the Seller Central Account. Instead, the option was introduced in the new books section, allowing booksellers to go against Amazon on this area. The Buy Box option was very affected by the price wars that took place on Amazon in the past year. A recent study shows that there is a link between high prices, algorithmic repricing, and getting the Buy Box.

It's fair to say that once you opt for Buy Box, you will not have it forever since you can lose this privilege at any time. Amazon puts different merchants to compete against each other, and it determines how long the reseller should hold on to it for a specific product. There were situations when a merchant was holding this option for the 70% of the day, leaving the remaining 30% to other resellers. The rule of thumb is that if a reseller is stronger than the rest, they will all share the Buy Box.

If you are having mid-metrics, then you will need to concentrate on a more competitive pricing. There is no mathematical formula that can guide you when it comes to getting Buy Box.

You are probably thinking:

- Isn't this only applicable if I'm going against other third-party merchants?

- What happens when I'm competing against Amazon itself?

- Does Amazon have its own customer performance metrics?

Although it's very difficult to beat Amazon at this game, it is still not impossible. With excellent metrics and very low prices, you have a chance of sharing Buy Box with them. If you are wondering what the criteria for this feature are, you can find them below.

Professional Seller Account

You can merely be eligible for Buy Box if you own a Professional Seller account (or what is called in Europe as a Pro-Merchant account). Individual sellers (Basic account users in Europe) can access this feature as well.

Buy Box eligibility status can be verified on the Amazon Seller Account.

New Items

Sellers of used products simply don't win the Buy Box because the item on sale must always be new. Any used items can be purchased from a separate section called Buy Used Box.

Availability

You need to have the listed product on the stock; otherwise, you will merely steer Buy Box towards a different merchant.

Since Buy Box is a temporary option, you will need to focus on finding alternatives to sell on Amazon. Some other ideas include going to other sellers on Amazon or the offer listings page. These two techniques may not be very profitable, but they are still credible and make the products visible enough.

The Other Sellers on Amazon option is located under the Buy Box, and it shows three distinct listings. Although they are not as obvious as the latter, there are still excellent alternatives for conversions.

The Offer Listing Place is a landing page where you can see different sellers with specific products, even though they don't have the Buy Box option. The order of listings is determined by the landing price, which is the product rate plus shipping costs. This page also offers details related to feedback, as well as delivery details and rebate terms.

In the past years, it looks like most of the purchases on Amazon were made using mobile devices. Just in the holiday period of 2016, 72% of the purchases were done digitally, and this is a continuously increasing trend.[15] In the mobile version of the platform, the Buy Box is displayed directly under the product image. Making purchases from handheld devices is a lot more direct approach because the mobile version does not display the Other Sellers or Offer Listing Place section. Therefore, it only shows the product connected to Buy Box. That means that plenty of merchants can't have their merchandise visible on the mobile version of Amazon. Since a majority of purchases is done through smartphones or tablets, getting the Buy Box should be your top priority.

There are four metrics that influence how a seller can obtain Buy Box: the fulfillment method (FBA), the Seller Fulfilled Prime, the landed price, and the delivery period. Fulfillment by Amazon is considered to have the best metrics across variables and is also the easiest way to get the Buy Box. Fulfillment by merchant (FBM) will never be able to do that; that's why it can never beat FBA. Seller Fulfilled Prime is an option provided by Amazon for the most performant FBM resellers, which practically offers them the benefits of Amazon Prime membership. Seller Fulfilled Prime can be very advantageous for this type of merchant as they have absolute control over their shipment

---

[15] Wallace, T., Goldwin, C., Thomson, J., et al. (2019). The definitive guide to selling on Amazon. BigCommerce (p. 78).

(while avoiding FBA fees) and get significantly increased chances of getting Buy Box.

The landed price represents the sum between the product and shipping costs. The general rule, in this case, is that the lower, the better. Meaning, lower landing prices will improve your opportunity of obtaining the Buy Box. However, there are a few exceptions if you have excellent performance metrics. For instance, you can have a higher landing price than your competition and still get the Buy Box. If other competitors have better metrics than you, then a lower landed price can help you obtain the Buy Box. When it comes to delivery times, lower delivery times will increase your chances of getting the Buy Box. If you can deliver within 48 hours, then you are eligible for this option.

Other metrics can still affect your chances of getting the Buy Box. They include on-time delivery, late shipment rate, order defect rate, valid tracking rate, the score from your feedbacks, number of feedbacks, and customer response time. The metrics with the lowest impact on the Buy Box are cancellation rate, refund rate, and inventory depth.

When you are using the Amazon platform, you are exposing your products in a very competitive environment and need to adjust your prices and always keep an eye on the competitors' prices. There are three distinct methods to adjust the rates on this platform.

1. **Manual repricing** actually means manually adjusting the prices for each ASIN. It can be the best option for the resellers of crafts and handmade products, but it may not be the best alternative in case you are selling competitive goods. The bigger your business is, the more inefficient and time-consuming this method gets.

2. **Repricing based on a rule** is a method that involves analyzing the price of your competitors and adjusting your prices according to previously set rules. You can choose to have a price lower than your rivals by a certain amount or stick to the low-price range. Even if it's better than the manual repricing, it still has some major flaws. The method is kind of limited because you are only looking at the prices of your competitors, as well as the amount of time that you spend on setting the rules. There is also the possibility of the rules being in conflict with each other, and this constitutes a more excessive management. This can be a total waste of time if your competitors have better metrics and still get the Buy Box, which means they can afford higher prices. A devastating consequence of using this method is the pricing wars, which can drag down prizes, decrease

the profits or even create losses for those ones engaged in this war.

3. **Algorithmic repricing** is a very good and sophisticated way to reprice your products as it takes into consideration all the possible variables that can influence your chances of getting the Buy Box. It merely monitors a lot of important factors and makes sure that your price is sustainable and capable of delivering profits without affecting your chance to get the Buy Box. So far, this software technology has delivered the best results and ROI for the merchants, and it also involves a lot less effort. Although this is by far the priciest option for pricing, it can still be used if you are aiming high or getting big profits.

There is no guaranteed method to obtain the Buy Box; instead, it comes with a bunch of metrics which impact your chances of getting this privilege. As mentioned above, the most important ones are Fulfillment by Amazon, Seller Fulfilled Prime, landed price, and delivery period. Improving your customer support service and finding the best practice to adjust your prices can significantly boost your chances of getting the Buy Box.

Chapter 5: What Are the Best Ways to Launch Your Products?

Reviews Are Extremely Important

One of the most influential factors when it comes to sales are the reviews. If optimizing and advertising play a decisive role in making the product more visible and boosting the rankings, reviews are responsible for increasing the conversion rate. Shoppers are constantly looking for information regarding a merchandise, after all. Having a well-structured product description is a big plus because the buyers can find important details related to the goods, such as specifications and a nicely written description. If you can write it as a story, that is a bigger bonus. What they also want to find is the opinion of other buyers regarding your product. The reviews are valid social statements connected to your merchandise; in many cases, the shoppers consider them the most trustworthy. A few things that you can see in a customer's feedback are:

- user experience

- shipping

- quality of the product

The specialist reviewers like to write them as a list of

advantages and disadvantages. They usually cover the points mentioned above, primarily if the product is user-friendly and it meets the customer's expectation related to quality and design, along with the delivery process itself. As users pop on this platform with a clear intention to buy products, the reviews are most influential when taking the decision to buy a product, assuming that the description and specifications already meet the buyer requirements. The more feedback you get, the more likely your product will sell. The A9 algorithm sees the reviews as extremely important, and it indexes them accordingly. As soon as you get your first review, this will mean an impressive boost in rankings. If you conduct your business in a niche with less competition, around ten to 20 sales should guarantee a spot for your product in the first two pages. Some merchants realized the importance of the reviews and tried to obtain them "artificially" by paying individuals to write reviews of products. This practice is not accepted by Amazon because it creates a fake image of a merchandise in front of customers. They have extremely strict terms and conditions related to this practice, but you can still find some tools to get honest reviews. Customers come first in Amazon's view; that's why they are focusing on achieving their satisfaction and protecting them from products of poor quality. If shoppers always consult the reviews when buying a merchandise online, merchants should also do that to improve the quality of their products and services. By listening to your customers (and consumers of your competitors), you can adjust and customize your products and services according to the needs of your customers. Sales may win you some people once, but the customer service and the quality of your product will give you their absolute loyalty. If you consider Amazon Retail, most of their consumers only use this platform to buy a broad range of products. They do not need to look anywhere else because they are extremely satisfied with the services and products provided by Amazon. At a lower scale, this is what you need to aim for. Furthermore, respecting the "voice" of your customers expressed through the reviews can undoubtedly help you achieve this objective.

Find Something to Boost Your Initial Sales

Let's consider that you are completely new to Amazon and want to make good money by selling high-quality goods to different buyers. At this point, you have the listings prepared, your content is optimized with keywords used in a natural manner, and you have very artistic photos well-structured and informative product description. However, you are still missing that special something to trigger your first sales. You know that you will be charged anyway by Amazon for your inventory, regardless if you make sales or not. As you are on this platform to sell goods, you can't afford to lose time so you need sales to start kicking immediately. In order to achieve this objective, besides optimizing your content, you will need to consider using Amazon Advertising to generate your first sales, particularly the Sponsored Products ads campaign. This involves setting buying special spots, which are extremely visible on the first page of results. It's also called Amazon PPC because you will place your product in that special spot, and you will pay for each click being made on your product. Since users are most likely interested to buy, they don't fool around when clicking on such an advertisement. If they like what they see, they will definitely buy a product. You need to set up your daily budget as well, which will cover a limited amount of clicks. This tool is your best chance of getting your first sales, making your first money on Amazon, and starting your journey to the top of the rankings. All the important details related to this procedure can be found in a previous chapter of this book.

Amazon Coupons

It's really hard to refuse a product that comes with a discount, especially when you are already interested in it or it is similar to the items that you are into. An interesting sale strategy is to have the first products sold for a lesser price to attract more shoppers towards your product. Of course, you merely can't sell all your existent inventory at a reduced rate; that's why it's important to set a limited amount of items that you want to sell for a discount. This a good way to make potential customers aware of your brand's merchandise. Traffic on Amazon can also be generated by external sources, such as your social media or business website. You can post an ad on Facebook or send customized emails to your customers from the database that you already have to announce your presence on Amazon and give them special offers. You can sweeten the deal by throwing in an Amazon coupon that's designated to provide a discount on one of your listed products on the platform. If you are hoping to get your first sales using this process, and let's say you have a few Amazon Coupons to give away, then you need to work intensively on this marketing campaign. After all, your presentation will need to reach more and more potential customers to become very effective. It's only up to you to choose your default sales trigger - whether you want to advertise through social media, send plenty of emails to your existing customers, give away discount coupons or choose the Amazon PPC option. Advertising on the platform can reach a higher number of customers compared to using external sources and offering coupons.

Follow Up to Get a Feedback

The most effective sale is the one that generates feedback because it creates all the necessary conditions to climb up on rankings, increase product visibility, and eventually generate other sales. In the old days of trade, sales were done through recommendations as well. The "word of mouth" was spread, and more and more people were aware of a specific product and its advantages. Sales triggered other sales, in other words. Things are about the same when it comes to online selling platforms, considering reviews and feedback are proven methods to produce more sales. The ideal situation is to get either after every sale, but it is genuinely hard to think of a seller which has achieved this performance. Reviews and feedback boost the popularity of the product and brand awareness, and shoppers are most likely to buy famed items because they are already considered trustworthy. A piece of good advice is to follow up with the customer to find out what he or she thinks about the merchandise. In the eyes of the shoppers, after all, it proves that you care about them and that you are willing to go the extra mile to satisfy their needs. This is the way to get positive feedback and reviews, which is something that Amazon and the users that are present on this platform appreciate very much. Another good idea is to comment on a customer review directly, thanking them for their opinion.

Chapter 6: How Can AMS Ads Help You?

Right from the beginning, you need to understand what AMS Ads stands for. It literally means Amazon Marketing Services ads - a service that has already been integrated into the Amazon Advertising methods. Placing advertisements on the platform is based on the cost-per-click (CPC) technique, while entails that every click made by users will amount to something. You can set the minimum value of the click at $0.02 or higher or make your daily or campaign budget as low as $1 or $100, respectively. Depending on your needs you can go a lot higher than that, but it is important to spend the money wisely using the standard bid or the Bid+ option (which was already discussed in a previous chapter of the book).

Amazon Marketing Services Ads are ads available to merchants who do not have a Seller Central account. The latter allows you to have Sponsored Product ads and use manual and auto-target keywords to promote your merchandise. Many Amazon specialists recommend both of them, although they focus more on the manual ones. Well, the AMS ads can be accessed through a Vendor Central account and allow you to use the manual-target keywords alone for the campaigns, thus showing the most significant difference between them. If Sponsored Products ads are available on several other marketplaces, AMS ads are merely accessible in the US, UK, and more recently Canada.

AMS ads is based on ad copy, which is a specific keyword-driven technique to generate more traffic to your website. Of all the spots where you can place an ad using this method, the Headline Search and the Display Product ads are probably the most important ones. The former is shown on top of the page, just above the organic search results. It' is an exact or almost exact match of a search term entered by the consumer. In other words, what he or she types should show up in your title or headline. It can generate traffic to your brand page, the bestselling products page or a custom link. The purpose of Headline Search ads is to produce less friction; that's why it is a product-based campaign. It's recommended to lure the traffic to a custom link where the shopper can find the exact product that he or she is looking for. The conversion rate should go through the roof with this option because this is a very useful type of targeted campaign.

Another interesting spot is Product Display ads, which can show up on your competitors' page, just above the Buy Box. In simpler terms, this option should show a link to your products just when the buyer is about to buy the product from your rivals. If you want, you can set this campaign to be interest-based so that it shows the consumers the other relevant products that they might need. This strategy may lower your conversion rate, but it should be able to help you sell other items. AMS ads was launched in 2012, but these days they are changing its name into Amazon Advertising Console.

Chapter 7: Setting Up an AMS Ads UK Account

As mentioned above, Amazon Marketing Services ads was named recently as Amazon Advertising Console. The basic features can be found in the previous chapter. Many of the accounts for this service are managed by agencies working for specific vendors. They are highly qualified and can run advertising campaigns for various sellers efficiently. However, to create an account with this AMS advertisements in the UK, you will need to follow the steps below:

1. Go to https://advertising.amazon.co.uk/.

2. Click on Register.

3. In the Sponsored Products and Sponsored Brands section, you can select "I Represent A Vendor" (assuming that you are an agency who works for the vendor).

4. You will be asked to create an Amazon account. It is recommendable to use a work email.

5. Next, you need to fill in the details section with information like brand name, contact name, email, phone number, and vendor code.

6. After submitting the details, it will take up to 48 hours until the account is approved. You will be informed via email when the approval process is over, and then you can start accessing the account.

Once you have access to the account, you will need to manage it using the following steps.

1. Ask the vendor to log in to this account.

2. Next, select "Manage Users" located in the drop-down menu just under the account name.

3. Then, the "Invite a new user" option will show up, which you have to fill in.

4. Soon, they should receive an email with the invitation to the account, gaining access to it. In the "Manage Users" section, you can remove users if you want.

Chapter 8: How to Get the Most Out of Amazon for Your Business?

Selling your own private-label products is probably the best option you can have on FBA to get the most success. Having this choice protects your inventory from other merchants who sell counterfeit products because you will significantly reduce the chances of your merchandise being commingled with the stocks of other resellers, which might not always be reliable.

You have to understand first what these private-label products are and how they can help you. They represent goods or services developed by one company, which are branded and sold by other companies. This is a popular practice among big retailers, such as Target's Mainstays, Walmart's Great Value Brand, and Amazon Essentials. Not only physical items can be considered private-label products; even varioustypes of services can be considered as such. Associating Fulfillment by Amazon with this feature can create one of the most powerful e-commerce tools that you can get online, and you can't wish for anything better.

You can find nine of the most important steps to success by using this method below.

1. Brainstorm product ideas

You will have to keep in mind that ideas can come from anywhere, so you don't have to ignore any potential sources of it. It is highly recommendable to check all kind of stores for popular products and then run market research on them to discover if the items in question can have an instant success online. You can visibly see this way if such a product can pose as an opportunity for you. Amazon can always be a very good source of inspiration since they have a dedicated section known as "Hot New Releases." Also, you can search in-depth through all the categories and subcategories and check the offer of other merchants on Amazon. The internet is also an infinite source of ideas (especially social media, where you can find pretty interesting and viral things) - it is definitely one that you should not ignore.

2. Keep the attributes of the product in mind

You have to consider the requirements that the product need to meet to become bestselling. Although they may be different from one category or subcategory to another, the ideal ones are:

- **Little with low weight**

  The product should fit into a small box with the dimensions of 8 11/16" x 5 7/16" x 1 ¾". It should not be heavier than one or two pounds as well. By sticking to these rules, you will not be charged extra by the carrier when shipping the product from the manufacturer or when you send it to the Amazon Fulfillmcnt Center.

- **Non-seasonal**

  The sales of your product should not be influenced by any season. Some seasonal product may include winter clothes, Christmas trees and decorations or Valentine's Day gifts.

- **Unchecked**

  You need to focus on selling products that don't require any special and additional paperwork to be imported and sold on Amazon. Toys have a very complicated situation because they are difficult to import and sell. Thus, it's important to stick with a merchandise that is easy to manufacture and distribute.

- **Effortless**

You will have to think of the after-sales process as well if you sell complicated products like electronics since handling customer service (the part not covered by Amazon) can be very challenging.

3. Conduct market research

Step 3 involves conducting market research on the products that you have discovered to be popular to find out if these items are worth selling or not. The good thing in this case is that you do not have to do spreadsheets manually. This saves you a lot of time and energy. There are a few tools that are extremely helpful for this process. One of them is the Jungle Scout Chrome Extension.

To make it work, you can start by performing a product search on Amazon using your own idea of a product. Open the Jungle Scout Chrome Extension from the right of the search/address bar by clicking on the "JS" button (considering you already purchased and downloaded the extension on Google Chrome). Check any data related to the merchandise, such as the statistics displayed by this tool that shows the average reviews per product or the average monthly sales.

It's up to you to establish the criteria that the product has to meet. Some specialists would probably look for items that have sales between 250 and 400 units per month. You do not want to get into fierce competition, though, so you will have to check the number of reviews for a product. If the average number of these reviews for such a product is below 100, then this is the niche market that you want to conduct business in.

4. Find out everything there is to know about product manufacturers and suppliers

Once you have determined that the product is worth selling, you need to find out where you can get it from. In order to be competitive, you have to have very low acquisition costs; that's why it matters to meet suppliers and manufacturers who can sell quality products at lower prices. Nowadays, everybody comes to China to look for low-priced items or raw materials. Thankfully, Alibaba can easily connect suppliers and manufacturers from China with merchants all over the world. The platform is safe enough to use, considering all the producers get verified before being allowed to function on this platform.

In order to get suppliers for your private-label products, you should follow the subsequent steps.

1. Register with a buyer account on www.alibaba.com.

2. Conduct an extensive search of the product that you are looking for. Don't worry about complexity

because this platform works like Amazon.

3. Get the listings that you want.

4. Contact the product supplier or manufacturer and demand for more information related to the product. You definitely need to find out the price per unit for bulk order (say, 500 items), as well as if the items can be shipped to your location. If so, you should inquire regarding the price for this service, payment terms and methods accepted, and other customizable options.

5. Work on your design, logo, and packaging

This aspect is no different from your business card because you have to dedicate time and get involved in this process. If you do not have any graphic design skills or tools available, you can always ask a freelancer to do this for you. Outsourcing the design and logo part to someone else can be a very good idea since you need to have them original. After all, you are creating a brand. When making the packaging, you might want to consider adding some contact details on it as well to improve your customer support service.

6. Decide on the fulfillment method

Depending on the volume of sales you are experiencing, you can select between Fulfillment by merchant (FBM) and Fulfillment by Amazon (FBA). If you are aiming for a high volume of sales, then the latter is your best choice. This option makes your merchandise available to Prime members, who are considered the big spenders and the most frequent shoppers on this platform. Also, it's easy to get better rankings by using this method.

7. Contract a manufacturer or supplier

By this point, you already know many aspects of your business, including offers from potential suppliers or manufacturers from Alibaba. The most important aspects to monitor at the beginning of the relationship with your new supplier are the delivery time, the condition of the sample upon arrival, and the ease of communication when tracking the delivery. These areas are probably more important than the cost itself because the supplier with the lowest cost probably does not provide the best quality of merchandise or is not very communicative when it comes to processing the items. You can also negotiate a lower pricing with the supplier that you have selected, motivating the lower price offered by other of its competitors. Afterward, you can agree on the payment terms and methods. PayPal is a frequently accepted method for suppliers on Alibaba.

8. Create your listings on Amazon

Once you have a contract with a manufacturer that you trust, you need to consider around three to four weeks until you get the products from them. You may also have to allocate at least a couple of weeks, considering that's how long it takes for the items to be sent to the Fulfillment Center. Therefore, you have to process everything from four to six weeks, which is more than enough to create your own listings on Amazon. You can't do this without having all the materials ready to be published or launched in advanced.

Also, make sure that you have photos of the highest quality. If you do not have the equipment or skills to make it happen, you should hire a professional photographer for your products. Another important aspect is to integrate the key features of the product into its description field and bullets section. Having a clearly structured description that contains keywords in a natural manner will make the product a lot more attractive in the eyes of the consumers, as well as influence them to buy your goods after clicking your link. If your private-label product meets their needs and expectations, then these consumers will most likely purchase your offerings.

9. Never stop optimizing your listings

The ultimate goal of your brand is to get higher rankings on the marketplace and seriously increase your sales. It is your job, therefore, to make sure that the products are more visible on the Amazon platform than ever to get more loyal customers. Sponsored Product ads is probably the most powerful tool to get traffic to your listings, but you also need to tweak your content with the best possible keywords to get more views and sales (conversions). There are plenty of tools to discover the keywords that your competitors are using, as well as find out which ones are trending the most. Once you have realized what these terms are, you will need to test them using different methods. Split testing (or commonly known as A/B testing) is one of the common techniques to find out what is working and what is not.

Among the most important aspects when using private-label products on this platform is the pricing. Many merchants focus on providing the lowest rates, but this strategy can prove to be a big mistake. Having the lowest price does not necessarily guarantee sales, but it can cut on your profit margin and give you less profit to reinvest in the future. You have to make your products more visible and accessible to customers through other methods instead. For instance, packaging, design, marketing language used in the title and description, and customer service experience. As a general rule, you will need to have the price 20% higher or lower than the average price displayed by your competitors. If the average price is \$25, then you shouldn't sell above \$30 or below \$20.[16] By respecting this rule, you will definitely increase your conversion rate.

Getting More and More Reviews

You can never say that you have enough reviews, considering selling on Amazon is a constant competition for selling more and getting the maximum amount of reviews. There is no surprise that people are buying the items with the most positive reviews on Amazon. They are often skeptical about trying a completely new product, a totally different one than the other goods they were used to. They need more information and assurance regarding it. Reviews play the role of social proof since it entails that somebody has already tried the product and that they have expressed their opinion about it. After checking all the reviews, they can get a glimpse about the quality and features of the merchandise. Fewer reviews also mean more risks because those feedback can't provide enough information to help a wise buyer to make a decision. Getting more honest reviews should be your main priority as a merchant, therefore, so that you can also set the right expectations for the future

---

[16] Wallace, T., Goldwin, C., Thomson, J., et al. (2019). The definitive guide to selling on Amazon. BigCommerce (p. 119).

buyers.

Amazon is a review-oriented platform. It values the customers and their opinions more than anything. A healthy way of growing your business on the marketplace is by asking the consumers to review a product after each sale. In return, you should reward them for expressing their opinion about the item. SEO optimization is a must on this platform because the environment is extremely competitive, and most of the products here have descriptions, reviews, suggested alternative products, and pricing.

Understanding how pricing works on Amazon is a key aspect that you can use in your favor. Running special discounts campaigns from time to time with very attractive offers can increase your brand awareness and entice more consumers to purchase your goods. Focusing on occasional discounts, getting the best reviews, and optimizing your content for SEO purposes will guarantee your success.

There is nothing more influential for customers than an impressive amount of positive reviews. This is what boost sales on the Amazon platform. If your product shows up high in the search results, then there is a tall chance for it to be sold as well. Of course, getting more sales and reviews is the ultimate goal, but how to achieve this objective is even more important. A feedback is also provided for items that you send out for free, and they are most likely positive in all cases. You can target the trusted influencers and reviewers and provide them with huge discounts in exchange for a review. They are willing to provide an objective opinion about the product and post it on the platform so that the customers can discover experts' feedback as well.

Generating Sales on Amazon

Although selling your products on Amazon with its brand on it can mean a lot in the eyes of the buyers, that is still not enough. You need to promote your merchandise and content by implementing marketing campaigns that are designed to influence the shopping habit of customers. Without advertising, you are not visible; that's why it matters to post your goods in the press or social media. A good option to increase the sales on Amazon is to use a range of marketing strategies to bring traffic to your listings and focus less on paid advertising. Use social networking sites and forums to steer traffic of hundreds of visitors to your listed products.

Setting the Right Prices

You need to stay out of strategic pricing to be protected from it. Therefore, when you list your products on Amazon, the customers will know that the price will remain at a certain level and will not have spectacular fluctuations. Personalized labelling can be very helpful as they can help you categorize items by rates. You can also rule out as many products as you want and prevent other merchants from your customers by providing cheaper prices for the merchandise that you also sell. You can still be ahead of your competition by not lowering the rate to a level that is no longer sustainable for you.

Basics of Amazon

Expanding your business on Amazon may be very complicated; that's why you have to be very cautious before proceeding. To be specific, you ought to ensure that you have the necessary resources to handle additional orders, so you need to order more from your supplier. It is crucial how you handle your inventory, so make sure that you use the right tools to keep track of your merchandise successfully. You need to avoid selling items which are out of stock as well or have your items delivered in time. Failing to do so will generate bad reviews from your customers, and you can even end up with your Amazon account suspended. A good piece of advice is to build a partnership with other brands or use Amazon as a testing marketplace for new products. In this case, you can team up with sports clubs, for instance, to develop a line of branded goods that can only be found on Amazon.

Chapter 9: Frequently Asked Questions

What does Fulfillment by Amazon represent?

Fulfillment by Amazon (FBA) is a very interesting option provided by this platform, which can help merchants boost their business by taking advantage of Amazon's expertise and resources, fast, free and trustworthy shipment, and outstanding customer support services. By choosing this option, you can send your inventory to the platform's warehouses (fulfillment centers) so that they can be stored over there and then leave everything to Amazon, including the picking, packing, and shipping of your customers' orders.

FBA is eligible for all the product categories and subcategories showing up on the Amazon Seller account. It is also available for any reseller who is curious to try it. The maximum weight limit for this program is 30 kilograms per product, so this is a requirement you need to know right from the start. You can test how your products are selling on Amazon, as well as send plenty of them to the fulfillment centers because you don't have to pay for anything upfront. You merely have to spend on their services that you use at the end of the month or when you make a sale.

What exactly is the Amazon Seller Central?

This is the type of account used by merchants, brands or sellers to manage and list their inventory on Amazon.

How to open an Amazon Seller Central account?

You need to establish the steps to follow when opening such an account:

- Select the products that you want to sell

- Visit services.amazon.com or sellercentral.amazon.com and click "Sell" on the main Amazon page.

- Select between the Professional and Individual selling plans.

- Register for the Amazon Seller account.

- Manage your account and list your products.

What are the fees involved when creating the Amazon Seller account?

When selecting the selling plan, you should be able to see the prices of both plans easily. The Individual account costs $0.99, while the Professional one amounts to $39.99. These are both monthly fees, and you are charged 30 days after the registration process.

Is it possible to create an Amazon Selling account for free?

Unfortunately, this is not an option on this platform because you need to choose between an Individual or Professional account.

What do I have to do in order to comply with Amazon's return policy?

Amazon will ask you to provide the following methods for returns:

- a return address;

- a prepaid return level; and

- a full refund without asking for the product to be returned.

How do consumers recognize the Fulfillment by Amazon products on the platform?

These products have the "Fulfillment by Amazon" logo, which provides the customers with the information that support service, returns, packing, and delivery are handled by Amazon.

How to label individual products?

When you wish to add your listings on the platform, you will be faced with a decision that can influence your further success on Amazon. To be precise, you have to select the labelling option, whether you want to send the products using EAN or UPC barcodes (these products fall into the Commingled Inventory or Stickerless category), or label the products properly (Labeled Inventory) to hide the original barcode completely. Commingled Inventory can be combined with other inventories from different merchants; that's why your customers might get products from different resellers, which may or may not have the same features as yours. Amazon will not open the boxes to check which product is the right one and from which merchant it has come from to ensure the authenticity of the merchandise. The Stickerless option, on the other hand, only refers to the products, not to the delivery. Although it may be a bit time-consuming and complicated, you may need to label the items well to protect your inventory and make sure that your customers are getting what they have ordered.

How to print labels for your own products?

When you are adding new products (inventory) from your Seller Central account (you will need to go into "Inventory Amazon Fulfils" and then "Send/replenish inventory") or just preparing an inventory, you are entering something called "shipping workflow." It will provide extra guidance on how to prepare your inventory to be shipped to Amazon's warehouses, thus giving you the option to customize the shipment considering the selections that you make during each step. At one point, you will be prompted to choose the labelling option and allow you to print your unit labels from the shipping workflow directly. These tags will include details like the product title, which can prove to be very helpful when it comes to matching the label with the right product. You need a printer and blank adhesive papers to print such labels, which can be found on the Amazon website or any store that sells office supplies.

Is there a possibility for Amazon to add the labels on your products?

This is a possible option, especially when you are entering the shipping workflow guide. You can simply select Amazon Label Service when prompted with the labelling options. This is a valid solution if you find the private label process too complicated and time-consuming.

How to pack products when sending them to Amazon?

You can find two different types of packing products before sending them to Amazon's warehouses below.

- Individually packed goods means that every box contains one or few units, depending on conditions and quantities.

- Packing items in a case is an option that will allow the merchant to place the products with the same SKU and condition into one box. The boxes will have the same quantity and the same item in them. When Amazon receives these boxes, they will only scan one item from the box and place the whole thing in your inventory. Amazon does not need to scan all the items, considering they are all the same.

When the reseller sends the products to Amazon, they can only be sent using one type of packing per shipment. Although they will be added to the inventory, if the merchant has individually packed items and cases with packed items, he or she will need to send them separately to Amazon.

How to choose a shipping method and carrier to send your inventory to Amazon?

The starting point of creating a new shipment is the "Send/replenish inventory" tab, which is present in the "Inventory Amazon Fulfils" section of your account. It is also possible when you have a work-in-progress inventory and you use the "shipping workflow" tool. By using the latter, you will receive step-by-step instructions on how to prepare your merchandise to be sent over to Amazon, including details about customizing your shipment according to the selections that you make at each step. One of them will allow you to choose from the shipping methods below:

- **Small Parcel Deliveries (SPDs)** represent individually packed and labelled products (one product per box), all prepared to be shipped.

- **Less-Than-Truckload (LTL)** shipments are, in fact, a mixed delivery because it contains pallets and individually boxed products. In this case, some of the products may be sent to different destinations, different warehouses.

- **Full Truckload (FTL)** also combines full pallets and individually packed products. The difference, however, is that the whole merchandise is going to one warehouse.

The FBA terms and conditions apply to all products that you send to and are meant to be sold on Amazon, regardless of the shipping method that you select. You can find more details related to how the platform receives and routes your products if you check these terms and conditions.

You can also choose a different carrier, other than the one provided by Amazon. Costs can be higher in this case, but if you do want to go ahead with this option, you will need to work with a trusted carrier that is capable of providing you with valuable information like a valid tracking number for SPD, the pro/freight bill number for FTL or LTL deliveries, and the bill of lading (BOL).

You can't send the inventory to Amazon using a privately-owned car, however. It can only be done by a registered carrier.

How to create shipping labels?

The shipping workflow is a sequence and tool where you can simply choose the type of labels that you want to have (if there is any). When selecting Small Parcel Delivery (SPD), you will be prompted to print shipping labels (just one per box) and packing slips. You will also need to place the packing slip inside the box, on the top side, so that it can be seen immediately after being opened at the Amazon's warehouse. The information that you should include are the destination and return addresses, while the label should be positioned just outside the sealed box as an addition to labels added by the carrier.

If you select Less-Than-Truckload, you still need to print a label per each box, which has to be placed outside of it so it can be seen when unwrapping the pallet. On the pallets, the tags have to be placed in a top-center position on each side (on the stretched wrap).

Adhesive labels can be found at any office supplies store or on Amazon.

Is it possible to arrange a shipment of inventory directly from an overseas supplier?

This is not an acceptable option because Amazon can't be used as the final address, importer or consignee when sending products from overseas. In this case, merchants will have to make the necessary arrangement to import and clear the shipment of customs. Only after doing this that they can send the inventory to Amazon's warehouses.

How to notify Amazon in advance regarding the products that I'm sending to them?

You have three options of sending products over to Amazon: Small Parcel Delivery (SPD), Less-Than-Truckload (LTL), and Full Truckload (FTL). For the last two choices, you will need to arrange delivery appointments; otherwise, the fulfillment centers may decline your shipment. In order to arrange a delivery appointment with the warehouse where you want to send the inventory, you will need first to download the Fulfillment by Amazon booking form, fill it, and email it to the carrier. In this form, you will have to place the ZIP code (you can find it in the Shipping Queue section of your account). Once the carrier has received your form, they will send it to the Amazon's Fulfillment Center to schedule the best delivery timing. It usually takes around 24 hours for the warehouse to reply back to the carrier with a confirmation for the delivery time.

How safe are Amazon's fulfillment centers?

You simply can't imagine better storage conditions for your inventory than the fulfillment centers owned by Amazon. hey are very secure and have the optimal temperature to keep your merchandise safe and in perfect condition. In many cases, picking, packing, and shipping tasks are done automatically, so they are all processed very fast. Some of the features of these establishments are 24/7 security staff, fully automated and wireless order tracking, climate-controlled storage units, and secured areas.

How are the feedbacks handled for any sold FBA product?

Leaving feedback is just a very powerful tool that buyers use on this platform to talk about a product. Amazon doesn't filter the feedback left by any buyer on FBA orders even if it's not related to the fulfillment part of the order.

In the case of poorly managed fulfillment caused by Amazon, which is reflected in the feedback left by the shopper, Amazon will be checking if: 1) the product in question is fulfilled by the platform; 2) the purchase rating of the buyer is between 1 and 3; 3) the buyer confirmed that the product is "Item as described"; and 4) the product did not arrive on time (according to the buyer).

Is Amazon taking care of refunds and customer returns for the FBA products?

Yes, but this is only valid for products sold on the platform! Amazon has its own policy when it comes to returns, and it is all included in the FBA Service Terms and Selling on Amazon Service Terms. They can merely process refunds and returns according to this policy. Any customer interested in returning an item that has been purchased from Amazon can check the Online Return Support Center where they can find contact details for the channel. Also, there is a designated Returns Center where all the customers who want to return a product will be directed. If it was not sold on the Amazon market, the merchant is solely responsible for the refund and return process.

What is the procedure in case of returns?

Well, this depends on the marketplace where the product was sold. If it was purchased on Amazon, and if they establish if the returned product can still be sold (meaning, it needs to have the same condition as before the sale), they will simply put the item back in your inventory and mark it as available for sale. If the merchandise is not in its original condition, Amazon will not place it back on sale, and the product will show up as "unfulfillable" in your account. At this point, you have 90 days to inform Amazon whether you want the product returned back to you or you just want it disposed of. If you fail to comply, Amazon will simply return the product to you.

In the case of a product being sold on a different platform, but it's fulfilled by Amazon, they will just send the product directly to you.

How to find the products which have been returned to Amazon and refunded to the customer?

When you use FBA with your Amazon Seller Central account, you can discover a reporting section from which you can download the report with returns requested by your customers.

If you are curious about refunds processed to your customers, you will need to check the payments sections of your account.

Can you consider Amazon as a search engine?

As it turns out, this platform also acts as a search engine.

There are plenty of situations in which the customers of this marketplace have the option to compare prices and find items that they might want to buy. With Alexa, for instance, the buyers have the option to use voice search instead of typing the query. Also, the platform can also be utilized to find out what new products are selling online.

Is Amazon's search algorithm updated regularly?

Nobody outside of Amazon knows for sure how often the search algorithm changes on this platform. Luckily for all the merchants selling over here, the current algorithm is quite stable, so you can optimize your content even if the system doesn't really change.

What does Amazon SERP stand for?

Every time you are searching for products on this platform, you can type in some keywords, and it acts as a search engine and displays a list of results. SERP is just the term used for these results because it literally means the search engine results page.

Conclusion

Amazon is perhaps the most competitive marketplace on the planet. It is a place where more than 2,000,000 merchants fight over 400,000,000 customers. The competition is extremely fierce, considering they have to go against each other and the platform itself. However, there are many resellers who stand as living proof of the success that they have achieved on this channel. Most of them are using a very interesting service provided on this platform called Fulfillment by Amazon. As discussed repeatedly in various chapters of this book, this service enables the merchant to use Amazon's infrastructure (warehouse and marketplace) to sell and store their merchandise. The platform favors the users of this service because of two different reasons. The first one is to make money (obviously). The second one is to help other sellers to have stellar delivery standards. After all, the Amazon shoppers deserve such level of standards when it comes to delivery and customer service. Some of the main perks provided by the FBA option include:

1. Eligibility for free delivery for the Prime members

In plenty of cases, the FBA products are associated with the Prime logo, which sends a strong message to the shopper:

the product can be shipped for free within 48 hours, and there are benefits that come with this subscription. Just in the US, there are more than 100,000,000 Prime members; that's why they are known as Amazon's big spenders and loyal shoppers. FBA products are exposed to this group, which offers the FBA merchant a great advantage over the others.

2. Amazon Coupons and Free Shipping

It is apparent that Amazon offers free shipping for products above $25 (regardless if the shopper is a Prime member or not). However, the truth is that most of the FBA products are already in this category. It's also the same when it comes to the Amazon coupons, in which case the FBA goods automatically qualify. They are, by definition, eligible products and, as mentioned in the description of free shipping, this service is applicable for them.

3. Better Rankings

FBA is a criteria that is taken into consideration by Amazon's A9 algorithm. This means that such goods are favored when listing the results, as well as getting better rankings and more sales. Every time Amazon displays results for a search term, the first two pages are the only ones with FBA products. The rest of the pages may not even matter for the average shopper on this platform.

4. Seriously Increased Chances of Getting Buy Box

The Buy Box option is the one that every merchant dream of getting because it promises the best placement on Amazon. This function enables easier sales of a specific product. FBA products have the highest priority in this case.

5. Trusted by Amazon

There is no better certificate for a merchant on the Amazon platform than its seal of approval. It's like a certificate of excellence, a proof that this merchant sells the best quality products and takes special care of their customers.

When it comes to shipping, FBA is the best option if you sell massively on Amazon or it is your main selling channel. The company puts its expertise on the table since the merchant using FBA will benefit from discounted carrier services, as well as professional customer support service related to product tracking, or returns. This is how you can benefit from top-notch services provided by Amazon. However, before rushing in to sign up for FBA, you need to know the costs first because this service doesn't come free of charge. There are fulfillment costs, storage fees (depending on the period your inventory sits in Amazon's warehouse), along with the amount that you need to pay for every sale. Not to mention that, in order to succeed and be at least one step ahead of your competitors, you have to seriously consider advertising as an option to boost rankings and sales (conversions).

Product sourcing is very important when you have to stay competitive, considering finding a supplier that can deliver high-quality and reasonably-priced products is a must. You can get a vague idea of the profit margin when you know the estimated price for which you will sell your products. If you have a merchandise that you know will sell and is not sold by many, you can do the math (estimate all the costs) and decide whether it is worth to go ahead with FBA.

If you decide to embark on the journey to win tons of money by selling on Amazon, then the FBA is definitely the right option to select. However, you can't hope to get high sales if your content is poor. You will need to optimize it, use keywords naturally, structure your product description very well, and include the key features of the product in there. Also, make sure to use high-quality pictures before launching your merchandise. Once you have the first sale, you will already notice that your rank is improving significantly, but you also have to pay attention to reviews to get as many as you can and take them into consideration to improve the quality of your products or provided services. Reviews are the most influential statements for any consumers since they can convert a simple view into sales. Everyone is on Amazon to sell; hence, the more you sell, the better. This should be the main objective for any merchant.

If you take all of the above into consideration, your chances of succeeding will increase significantly. Although this is a very competitive environment, there is no better place to sell products than Amazon. This is the place to be. You will need skills to implement every idea mentioned in the previous chapters, but it is genuinely not a shame to ask the advice of professionals, especially if they can help you to achieve your main objectives. A large of volume of sales is within your grasp, and it's only up to you to decide how much you want to sell and how visible you want to be to your potential customers. The only thing left to say is: Good luck!

References

Amazon Advertising. (n.d.). Retrieved from https://advertising.amazon.com/

Cracked. (2016). I get paid to write fake reviews for Amazon. Retrieved from https://www.cracked.com/personal-experiences-2376-i-get-paid-to-write-fake-reviews-amazon.html

Reisinger, D. (2019). Amazon Prime has 100 million U.S. members. Retrieved from http://fortune.com/2019/01/17/amazon-prime-subscribers/

Robischon, N. (2017). Why Amazon Is the world's most innovative company of 2017. Retrieved from https://www.fastcompany.com/3067455/why-amazon-is-the-worlds-most-innovative-company-of-2017

Smith, C. (2019). 150 amazing Amazon statistics and facts (2019) | By the numbers. Retrieved from expandedramblings.com/index.php/amazon-statistics/

Stim, R. (n.d.). What rights the first sale doctrine gives to a purchaser of a copywrighted work. Retrieved from https://www.nolo.com/legal-encyclopedia/the-first-sale-doctrine.html

United States Patent and Trademark Office. (n.d.). Trademark basics. Retrieved from https://www.uspto.gov/trademarks-getting-started/trademark-basics

Waber, A. (2018). 4 ways brands can win the digital shelf in 2018. Retrieved from https://marketingland.com/4-ways-brands-can-win-the-digital-shelf-in-2018-236906

Wallace, T., Goldwin, C., et al. (2019). The definitive guide to selling on Amazon. BigCommerce (p. 68, 74, 78, 92, 119, 122, 179, 187).

Made in the USA
Middletown, DE
16 August 2019